PERGAMON INSTITUTE OF ENGLISH (OXFORD)

Language Teaching Methodology Series

SECOND LANGUAGE ACQUISITION

AND

SECOND LANGUAGE LEARNING

D1300137

Other titles in this series include:

See also SYSTEM: *the International Journal of Education Technology and Language Learning Systems* (sample copy available on request)

SECOND LANGUAGE ACQUISITION

AND

SECOND LANGUAGE LEARNING

STEPHEN KRASHEN
University of Southern California

PERGAMON PRESS
OXFORD · NEW YORK · TORONTO · SYDNEY · PARIS · FRANKFURT

U.K.	Pergamon Press Ltd., Headington Hill Hall, Oxford OX3 0BW, England
U.S.A.	Pergamon Press Inc., Maxwell House, Fairview Park, Elmsford, New York 10523, U.S.A.
CANADA	Pergamon Press Canada Ltd., Suite 104, 150 Consumers Road, Willowdale, Ontario M2J 1P9, Canada
AUSTRALIA	Pergamon Press (Aust.) Pty. Ltd., P.O. Box 544, Potts Point, N.S.W. 2011, Australia
FRANCE	Pergamon Press SARL, 24 rue des Ecoles, 75240 Paris, Cedex 05, France
FEDERAL REPUBLIC OF GERMANY	Pergamon Press GmbH, Hammerweg 6, D-6242 Kronberg-Taunus, Federal Republic of Germany

P5I
K66
1981

First edition 1981
Reprinted 1983, 1984

British Library Cataloguing in Publication Data
Krashen, Stephen
Second language acquisition and second language
learning. — (Language teaching methodology series).
1. Language and languages — Study and teaching
I. Title   II. Series
401'.9   P53   80-40815
ISBN 0-08-025338-5

Printed in Great Britain by A. Wheaton & Co. Ltd., Exeter

Acknowledgments

I would like to thank the following journals and organizations for granting permission to reprint material: Newbury House, the Center for Applied Linguistics, *Language Learning*, TESOL, the *SPEAQ Journal*, Academic Press.

I have had a great deal of help and feedback from many people in writing this book. Among the many scholars and friends I am indebted to are Marina Burt, Earl Stevick, Heidi Dulay, Robin Scarcella, Rosario Gingras, Nathalie Bailey, Carolyn Madden, Georgette Ioup, Linda Galloway, Herbert Seliger, Noel Houck, Judith Robertson, Steven Sternfeld, Batyia Elbaum, Adrian Palmer, John Oller, John Lamendella, Evelyn Hatch, John Schumann, Eugene Brière, Diane Larsen-Freeman, Larry Hyman, Tina Bennet, Ann Fathman, Janet Kayfetz, Ann Peters, Kenji Hakuta, Elinor Ochs, Elaine Andersen, Peter Shaw, and Larry Selinker. I also would like to express my thanks to those scholars whose work has stimulated my own thinking in the early stages of the research reported on here: John Upshur, Leonard Newmark, and S. Pit Corder all recognized the reality of language "acquisition" in the adult long before I did. I would also like to thank Eula P. Krashen and Judy Winn-Bell Olson for their special contributions.

Contents

Introduction

This book is concerned with what has been called the "Monitor Theory" of adult second language acquisition. Monitor Theory hypothesizes that adults have two independent systems for developing ability in second languages, subconscious language *acquisition* and conscious language *learning,* and that these systems are interrelated in a definite way: subconscious acquisition appears to be far more important.

The introduction is devoted to a brief statement of the theory and its implications for different aspects of second language acquisition theory and practice. We define acquisition and learning, and present the Monitor Model for adult second language performance. Following this, brief summaries of research results in various areas of second language acquisition serve as both an overview of Monitor Theory research over the last few years and as introduction to the essays that follow.

Acquisition and Learning and the Monitor Model for Performance

Language *acquisition* is very similar to the process children use in acquiring first and second languages. It requires meaningful interaction in the target language—natural communication—in which speakers are concerned not with the form of their utterances but with the messages they are conveying and understanding. Error correction and explicit teaching of rules are not relevant to language acquisition (Brown and Hanlon, 1970; Brown, Cazden, and Bellugi, 1973), but caretakers and native speakers can modify their utterances addressed to acquirers to help them understand, and these modifications are thought to help the acquisition process (Snow and Ferguson, 1977). It has been hypothesized that there is a fairly stable order of acquisition of structures in language acquisition, that is, one can see clear

1

similarities across acquirers as to which structures tend to be acquired early and which tend to be acquired late (Brown, 1973; Dulay and Burt, 1975). Acquirers need not have a conscious awareness of the "rules" they possess, and may self-correct only on the basis of a "feel" for grammaticality.

Conscious language *learning*, on the other hand, is thought to be helped a great deal by error correction and the presentation of explicit rules (Krashen and Seliger, 1975). Error correction, it is maintained, helps the learner come to the correct mental representation of the linguistic generalization. Whether such feedback has this effect to a significant degree remains an open question (Fanselow, 1977; Long, 1977). No invariant order of learning is claimed, although syllabi implicitly claim that learners proceed from simple to complex, a sequence that may not be identical to the acquisition sequence.

The fundamental claim of Monitor Theory is that conscious learning is available to the performer only as a *Monitor*. In general, utterances are initiated by the acquired system—our fluency in production is based on what we have "picked up" through active communication. Our "formal" knowledge of the second language, our conscious learning, may be used to alter the output of the acquired system, sometimes before and sometimes after the utterance is produced. We make these changes to improve accuracy, and the use of the Monitor often has this effect. Figure 1 illustrates the interaction of acquisition and learning in adult second language production.

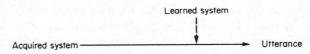

Fig. 1. Model for adult second language performance

The acquisition–learning distinction, as I have outlined it, is not new: Lawler and Selinker (1971) propose that for rule internalization one can "postulate two distinct types of cognitive structures: (1) those mechanisms that guide 'automatic' language performance . . . that is, performance . . . where speed and spontaneity are crucial and the learner has no time to consciously apply linguistic mechanisms . . . and (2) those mechanisms that guide puzzle- or problem-solving performance . . ." (p. 35). Corder (1967), citing an unpublished paper by Lambert, also discusses the acquisition–learning distinction and the possibility that acquisition is available to the adult second language performer.

The Monitor Theory differs somewhat from these points of view, in that it makes some very specific hypotheses about the inter-relation between acquisition and learning in the adult. In the papers that follow, I argue that this hypothesis sheds light on nearly every issue currently under discussion in second language theory and practice.

Conditions of Monitor Use

There are several important constraints on the use of the Monitor. The first condition is that in order to successfully monitor, the performer must have *time*. In normal conversation, both in speaking and in listening, performers do not generally have time to think about and apply conscious grammatical rules, and, as we shall see later, we see little or no effect on the Monitor in these situations. This condition, however, is necessary but not sufficient. Heidi Dulay and Marina Burt have pointed out to me that a performer may have time but may still not monitor, as he or she may be completely involved with the message. There is, thus, a second condition: the performer must be "focused on form", or correctness. As we shall see later, the second condition predicts some recent data nicely.

An important third condition for successful Monitor use is that the performer needs to know the rule, he or she needs to have a correct mental representation of the rule to apply it correctly. This may be a very formidable requirement. Syntacticians freely admit that they have only analyzed "fragments" of natural languages, applied linguists concede that they have mastered only part of the theoretical literature in grammar, language teachers usually do not have the time to fully study the descriptive work of all applied linguists, and even the best language students do not usually master all the rules presented to them.

It is therefore very difficult to apply conscious learning to performance successfully. Situations in which all three conditions are satisfied are rare (the most obvious being a grammar test!).

Note that the model presented here allows us to self-correct using acquired knowledge of language, or our "feel" for grammaticality. That is what native speakers generally do in the case of speech errors. The point is not that we can only monitor using conscious rules. This is not the case. The point is that conscious learning is only available as a Monitor.

In the last few years, the acquisition–learning distinction has been shown to be useful in explaining a variety of phenomena in the field of second language acquisition. While many of these phenomena may have alternative explanations, the claim is that the Monitor Theory provides for all of them in a general, non *ad hoc* way that satisfies the intuitions as well as the data. The papers in this volume review this research, and include discussion of how the second language classroom may be utilized for both acquisition and learning.

Individual Variation

Chapter 1, based on a paper written in 1976 and published in Ritchie (1978), describes how the learning–acquisition distinction captures one sort of individual variation in second language performance. Based on case histories, this section proposes that there are basically three types of performer:

Monitor "overusers" are performers who feel they must "know the rule" for everything and do not entirely trust their feel for grammaticality in the second language. One case, "S", described by Stafford and Covitt (1978), remarked: "I feel bad . . . when I put words together and I don't know nothing about the grammar." In Stevick's terms (Stevick, 1976, p. 78), overusers may suffer from "lathophobic aphasia", an "unwillingness to speak for fear of making a mistake".

At the other extreme is the underuser, who appears to be entirely dependent on what he can "pick up" of the second language. Underusers seem to be immune to error correction, and do not perform well on "grammar" tests. They may acquire a great deal of the target language, however, and often use quite complex constructions.

The optimal user is the performer who uses learning as a real supplement to acquisition, monitoring when it is appropriate and when it does not get in the way of communication (e.g. prepared speech and writing). Very good optimal users may, in fact, achieve the illusion of native speaker competence in written performance. They "keep grammar in its place", using it to fill gaps in acquired competence when such monitoring does not get in the way of communication.

Attitude and Aptitude

Chapter 2 illustrates how the acquisition–learning hypothesis provides a parsimonious explanation for what had appeared (to me) to be a mysterious finding: both language aptitude, as measured by standard language aptitude tests, and language attitude (affective variables) are related to adult second language achievement, but are not related to each other.

This section explores two hypotheses that attempt to account for this problem. The first is that aptitude may be directly related to conscious learning (especially certain components, as detailed in Chapter 2). As we shall see in Chapter 2, scores on aptitude tests show a clear relationship to performance on "monitored" test situations and when conscious learning has been stressed in the classroom.

Second language attitude refers to acquirers' orientations toward speakers of the target language, as well as personality factors. The second hypothesis is that such factors relate directly to acquisition and only indirectly to conscious learning. Briefly, the "right" attitudinal factors produce two effects: they encourage useful input for language acquisition and they allow the acquirer to be "open" to this input so it can be utilized for acquisition.

The pedagogical implications of these hypotheses will not surprise many experienced teachers: if the direct relationship between acquisition and attitudinal factors does exist, and if our major goal in language teaching is the development of communicative abilities, we must conclude that attitudinal factors and motivational factors are more important than aptitude. This is because conscious learning makes only a small contribution to communicative ability.

Chapter 2 also contains a discussion of the nature of child–adult differences, claiming that the Monitor, the conscious grammar, may owe its source to Piaget's Formal Operations stage. Affective changes that occur around puberty, some related to Formal Operations, affect language acquisition. The chapter concludes with a re-definition of the "good language learner", now defined as someone who is first and foremost an acquirer, and who may also be an "optimal Monitor user".

Chapter 2 originally appeared in Diller (1980).

Formal and Informal Linguistic Environments

Chapter 3 is a revised version of a paper that appeared in the *TESOL Quarterly* in 1976 (see Krashen, 1976a). It shows how the acquisition–learning distinction helps to solve a puzzle in the second language acquisition research literature: several studies apparently show that formal learning environments are best for attaining second language proficiency, while other studies appear to show that informal environments are superior. In this section, it is argued that informal environments, when they promote real language use (communication), are conducive to acquisition, while the formal environment has the potential for encouraging both acquisition and learning.

This chapter, then, begins the discussion of the potential of the second language classroom for language acquisition, a discussion that is continued in later sections (Chapters 8 and 9).

The Domain of the Conscious Grammar: The Morpheme Studies

Chapter 4 reviews research pertaining to acquisition or difficulty order of certain structures, that is, which structures adult second language acquirers tend to acquire early and which they tend to acquire late.

The value of these studies is considerable. They provide more information than merely showing us the actual order of acquisition. They also show us when performers are using conscious grammar and when they are not. We have hypothesized that when conditions for "Monitor-free" performance are met, when performers are focused on communication and not form, adult errors in English as a second language (for grammatical morphemes in obligatory occasions[1]) are quite similar to errors made by children acquiring English as a second language (some similarities to first language acquisition have been noted as well). When second language speakers "monitor", when they focus on form, this "natural order" is disturbed. The appearance of child-like errors in Monitor-free conditions is hypothesized to be a manifestation of the acquired system operating in isolation, or with little influence of the Monitor.

Current research in the "morpheme studies" supports the hypothesis that second language performers utilize the conscious grammar extensively only when they have to do extreme "discrete-point" grammar tests, tests that test knowledge of rules and vocabulary in isolation.

Also included in Chapter 4 is a response to some criticisms of the morpheme studies. Material in Chapter 4 was previously published in Gingras (Krashen, 1978b) and in a paper appearing in *On TESOL '77* (Krashen, 1977a).

The Role of the First Language

Chapter 5 deals with so-called first language "interference". It attempts to provide some empirical data for a position first held by Newmark (1966): "interference" is not the first language "getting in the way" of second language skills. Rather, it is the result of the performer "falling back" on old knowledge when he or she has not yet

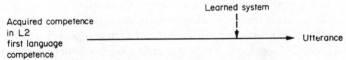

Fig. 2. First language influence in second language performance

acquired enough of the second language. In terms of the Monitor performance model, interference is the result of the use of the first language as an utterance initiator: first language competence may replace acquired second language competence in the performance model, as in Fig. 2.

From the data we have so far, this hypothesis correctly predicts that those aspects of syntax that tend to be acquired are also those that show first-language-influenced errors in second language performance.

First language influence may thus be an indicator of low acquisition, or the result of the performer attempting to produce before having acquired enough of the target language. It is, not surprisingly, found most often in foreign language, as opposed to second language situations, where opportunities for real communication are fewer, and is only rarely seen in "natural" child second language acquisition. Children are usually allowed to go through a "silent period", during which they build up acquired competence through active listening. Several scholars have suggested that providing such a silent period for all performers in second language acquisition would be beneficial (see, for example, Postovsky, 1977).

Note that it is possible for performers to use the first language and the Monitor to perform without any aquired competence in the second language. This bizarre mode is severely limited, yet its use may give the adult a temporary head-start over children, who presumably rely on acquisition alone for the most part.

This chapter is a slightly expanded version of a paper that originally appeared in *On TESOL '77* (Krashen, 1977a).

Neurological Correlates

Chapter 6 was originally published in the *SPEAQ Journal*, co-authored with Linda Galloway (Krashen and Galloway, 1978). It discusses current research in two areas of neurolinguistics and the relationship of this research to the acquisition–learning hypothesis. The first part of this chapter deals with the development of cerebral dominance, and explores research bearing on Lenneberg's hypothesis that child–adult differences in second language acquisition are due to the completion of the development of cerebral dominance, hypothesized by Lenneberg to occur at around puberty. More recent reports place the completion of the development of cerebral dominance much earlier (some claiming age 5, others claiming that laterality is present at birth). The implications of this research are that the "critical period" and cerebral dominance may not be related at all. Other explanations of child–adult differences are discussed, namely the hypothesis presented in Chapter 2, that Formal Operations causes an increase in our ability to *learn* but damages our ability to *acquire*.

In the second part of this chapter, the role of the right hemisphere in language acquisition is discussed. Psychological and neurological evidence is presented in support of the hypothesis that there is an early stage in second language acquisition (not learning) that involves the right side of the brain. Since it may be the case that early first language acquisition also involves some right hemisphere participation, confirmation of such a hypothesis would strengthen the parallel between first and second language acquisition.

Routines and Patterns

Chapter 7 originally appeared in *Language Learning* and was co-authored with Robin Scarcella.

Routines and patterns are "memorized language". Routines are whole sentences or phrases, such as *How are you?*, and patterns are sentence frames with open slots, such as *That's a* ———. A performer can use routines and patterns without learned or acquired knowledge of its internal parts. This chapter presents evidence to support the hypothesis that routines and patterns are fundamentally different from both acquired and learned language, and they do not "turn into" acquired or learned language directly. This evidence is drawn from neurolinguistic research, and studies in child first, child second, and adult language acquisition. Routines and patterns may be quite helpful, however, in establishing and maintaining social relations, and managing conversations, as Fillmore's work points out.

Theory to Practice

Chapter 8 deals directly with application to the second language classroom. It focuses, first of all, on the important question of how we acquire, concluding that *comprehensible input* is the crucial and necessary ingredient. This hypothesis, the "Input Hypothesis", is discussed in more detail in Chapter 9. I then discuss what sorts of activities provide comprehensible input, input language in which the focus is on the message and not the form.

This chapter is optimistic with respect to the role and value of the classroom in encouraging second language acquisition, suggesting that the classroom should be viewed as a place where the student can get the input he or she needs for acquisition. The classroom may be superior to the outside world for beginning and low intermediate students, in that the real world is often quite unwilling to provide such students with comprehensible input, as Wagner-Gough and Hatch have pointed out.

This section also discusses the possible role of conscious learning, pointing out that "easy" rules can be taught for optimal Monitor use, but that "hard" rules may only serve a "language appreciation" function for most students.

An earlier version of this chapter was published in the *SPEAQ Journal* (Krashen, 1978d) and in Felix (1980).

The Relevance of Simple Codes

The final chapter, Chapter 9, is the most recently written, and appeared in Scarcella and Krashen (1980). It focuses on the question of simplified input, both inside the classroom (i.e. teacher-talk) and outside the classroom (i.e. foreigner talk), asking whether such simplified input is of use to second language acquisition. The conclusion is that such input is not only highly useful, but it is possibly essential. Simple codes may provide for the second language acquirer what "caretaker speech" provides for the first language acquirer, comprehensible input with a low "affective filter".

Simple codes, input that the acquirer understands, are not deliberately grammatically sequenced or controlled. Rather, the speaker is only concerned with whether the listener understands the message. It is quite possible, it is argued, that the natural "net" of grammatical structures that such simple codes provide is an excellent natural syllabus, presenting a sufficient quantity of those structures the acquirer is "ready" to acquire, and allowing for built-in review.

The implications are as follows: the best language lessons may be those in which real communication takes place, in which an acquirer understands what the speaker is trying to say. Similarly, a reading passage is appropriate for a student if he or she understands the message. Finally, the teacher-talk that surrounds the exercises may be far more valuable than the exercise itself. We teach language best when we use it for what it was designed for: communication.

Note

¹ Correct use in obligatory occasions means simply that the acquirer supplied the morpheme where it was required. For example, the underlined portion of this sentence is an obligatory occasion for the plural morpheme in English:

   I have three pencil __ .

Analysis of grammatical morphemes in obligatory occasions was begun by Brown (1973). As indicated in Chapter 4, analysis in obligatory occasions does not give a complete picture of language acquisition. It does, however, provide valuable information on order of acquisition of grammatical items.

1. Individual Variation in the Use of the Monitor

The acquisition–learning distinction helps interpret findings in all areas in second language acquisition research and practice. One important area, the first we shall deal with, is the area of individual variation.

As discussed in the Introduction, one might suppose that individual second language performers would vary with respect to the extent to which they utilize the Monitor in second language production. At one extreme end of the continuum, some performers might utilize conscious knowledge of the target language whenever possible. Extreme Monitor users might, in fact, be so concerned with editing their output to make it conform to their conscious rules that fluency would be seriously hampered. At the other end of the continuum, we may find those who almost never monitor their output.

These sorts of individuals do exist, and their case histories are revealing, both as to the theoretical question regarding the operation of the Monitor Model, and with respect to the practical question of what role instruction should play in helping second language performers improve.

General Characteristics of Monitor Users

Before describing the extreme cases, we shall first turn to some typical instances of Monitor utilization in adult second language performance. Several informal case studies will be presented to illustrate some general characteristics of Monitor users, namely:

1. Successful Monitor users edit their second language output when it does not interfere with communication.
2. This editing results in variable performance, that is, we see different types and amounts of errors under different conditions.

12

Monitoring generally improves accuracy levels, and as we have noted above, under edited conditions, where attention is on form, we no longer see the child's "natural" difficulty order.
3. Monitor users show an overt concern with "correct" language, and regard their unmonitored speech and writing as "careless".

Case Studies of Monitor Users

An interesting case study, illustrating some of the points mentioned above, is P, a fairly typical successful Monitor user studied by Krashen and Pon (1975). P was a native speaker of Chinese in her 40s, who had begun to learn English sometime in her 20s when she came to the United States. About 5 years before she was studied by Krashen and Pon, she had enrolled in college, and had graduated with an "A" average.

Krashen and Pon studied P's casual, everyday language production. Observers, native speakers of English (usually P's son), simply recorded her errors from utterances she produced in normal family living or in friendly conversational situations. Immediately after an utterance containing an error was recorded, it was presented to the subject. The data were gathered over a 3-week period and about 80 errors were tabulated.

Upon considering P's self-correction behaviour, the investigators came to what was then an unexpected conclusion:

> We were quite surprised to note . . . that our subject was able to correct nearly every error in the corpus (about 95%) when the errors were presented to her after their commission. In addition, in nearly every case she was able to describe the grammatical principle involved and violated. Another interesting finding was that for the most part the rules involved were simple, "first level" rules (e.g. omission of the third person singular ending, incorrect irregular past tense form, failure to make the verb agree with the subject in number (is/are), use of "much" with countable nouns, etc.) (p. 126).

The fact that the vast majority of P's errors were self-correctable suggested that "she had a conscious knowledge of the rules" but did not choose to apply this knowledge. Further evidence that this is the case "is our observation that the subject is able to write a virtually error-free English. . . . In writing, and in careful speech, she utilizes her conscious linguistic knowledge of English, while in casual speech she may be too rushed or preoccupied with the message to adjust her output [p. 126]."

P thus illustrates the general characteristics of the successful Monitor user noted above. She is able to communicate well in both Monitor free and edited situations, applying the Monitor when it is appropriate to focus on form. Her performance is variable, in that she makes some errors in unmonitored speech, while her written output is quite close to the native speaker's norm. In a sense, she is able to achieve the illusion of the native speaker's syntactic level of performance by efficient, accurate monitoring.

Cohen and Robbins (1976) describe two more cases like this in their in-depth study of learner characteristics. Ue-lin, like P, can self-correct successfully, and describes her errors as "careless". She reports that she likes to be corrected and has the practice of going over teacher's corrections on her written work. Her background includes formal training in English.

Eva, also described by Cohen and Robbins, is also a Monitor user. Eva made the following statement, which appears to indicate a conscious awareness of Monitor use: "Sometimes I would write something the way I speak. We say a word more or less in a careless way. But if I take my time, sometimes go over it, that would be much easier. . . . Whenever I go over something or take my time, then the rules come to my mind [p. 58]." This statement is easily translated into the vocabulary of the Monitor Model. "Sometimes I would write something the way I speak" reflects the use of the acquired system in language production when monitoring is not involved. Eva's comments about the "carelessness" of her spoken language, which are similar to Ue-lin's statement, simply reflect the fact that ordinary casual speech is usually unmonitored. "The rules come to [her] mind" when she focuses on the form of her utterance ("whenever I go over something"), rather than just on its function as communication.

Until the creative construction process has completed its mission in the adult second language performer, the use of monitoring in edited language can certainly be an aid. The world often demands accurate language, even from second language users, in just those domains where Monitor use is most possible—in the written language—and a clear idea of linguistic rules can be a real asset for the performer. An overconcern with correctness, however, can be a problem. The overuser may be so concerned with form that he or she is unable to speak with any fluency at all.

The Overuser

Stafford and Covitt (1978) present an instructive case of a Monitor overuser: S, a Finnish speaker who, like P, knows many of the rules of English, but who is often unable to communicate in speech. While her written English is quite accurate, Stafford and Covitt remark that "she speaks very little, because she tries to remember and use grammar rules before speaking". S's self-correction behavior reveals her lack of faith in her acquired knowledge of English. Stafford and Covitt report that she generally does not trust her intuitions about English syntax but relies on conscious rules. S describes her own situation as follows: "I feel bad . . . when I put words together and I don't know nothing about the grammar."

Birnbaum (1976) characterizes the speech of Hector, another adult second language performer and ESL student who shows signs of overuse, as follows: "In a segment of conversation that lasted slightly less than fifteen minutes, there is not a single lengthy utterance that is not filled with pauses, false starts, repetitions, and other speech repairs. . . . There are over 69 . . . instances of repair (not counting pauses)." We are not surprised to learn that Hector's written English, his class compositions "produced in a situation where extreme monitoring is possible—are among the best in his section".

The Monitor overuser refers to his conscious grammar all the time, when using his second language. This may be due to an overconcern with correctness. "S", the overuser described by Stafford and Covitt (1978), who admitted that "I feel bad when I put words together and I don't know nothing about the rules", is clearly this sort. Mr. J., described by Nida (1956), also seems to be an overuser of this type. Mr. J., a missionary, became an expert in the grammar of his target language but never spoke it. Nida suggests that this may have stemmed from his early use of a nonprestige dialect of English and his efforts to learn the prestige form ("he felt he could not dare for a minute to make a 'mistake', thus exposing his background and running the risk of losing the position he had sought so hard to win'', p. 53).

Overuse of the Monitor can also stem from a simple lack of acquisition. Those trained only in foreign language classrooms, where the emphasis was on conscious grammar, may develop extensive formal knowledge of the target language, with very little acquisition, and consequently have no choice but to be overusers. Such performers may utilize the first language as an utterance initiator when forced to speak, since they lack acquired competence in the second language.

Overusers, regardless of type, will typically self-correct ''by rule'', that is, when correcting errors, they will often be consciously aware of the rule that was broken and be able to verbalize it. (Such reactions are documented in the literature: Cohen and Robbins, 1976; Krashen, 1978a; Krashen and Pon, 1975; Krashen, Robertson, Loop, and Rietmann, 1977.)

Overusers also typically have a hesitant, overcareful style of speaking, thanks to their overconcern with correctness and constant rule-searching.

The Underuser

At the other extreme are adult second language performers who do not seem to use a monitor to any extent, even when conditions encourage it. Such performers, like first language acquirers, appear to be uninfluenced by most error correction and do not usually utilize conscious linguistic knowledge in second language performance.

The Monitor underuser does not seem to use the conscious grammar at all. The underuser typically judges grammaticality ''by feel'', that is, he uses his subconsciously acquired system, rather than a conscious grammar. Several performers described in the literature appear to be underusers, such as Hung, described by Cohen and Robbins. Hung was quoted as saying:

> I never taught any grammars. I guess I just never learned the rules that well. I know that every time I speak it's pretty correct, so I never think about grammars. I just write down whatever I feel like it. Everytime I write something I just stop thinking. I don't know which (rule) to apply . . . (p. 59).

The underuser may be living in the country where the target

language is spoken or may be exposed to frequent use of the second language in his own country. Many immigrants who haphazardly attend adult second language classes are typical of this type. It is interesting to note that underusers may control impressive amounts of the target language without the benefit of conscious rules.

Stafford and Covitt describe several cases of Monitor underusers, and make the interesting point that underusers may pay lip service to the importance of linguistic rules but in reality may hardly use them at all. First consider the case of V, an ESL student whom they depict as "verbal and energetic". V values the study of grammar very highly. On a questionnaire administered by Stafford and Covitt, he wrote, "Grammar is the key to every language." V thinks he uses conscious rules in performance—"When I know a grammar rule, I try to apply it"—but careful questioning reveals that V actually knows few rules and self-corrects "by feel". The following exchanges, taken from a conversation between V and one of the investigators, illustrate this:

> Int.: [When you write a composition] . . . do you think of grammar rules? Do you think "Should I have used the present tense here or would the present continuous be better or . . ."
> V: I don't refer that to the books and all that, you know. I just refer it to this uh, my judgment and . . . sensing it if I'm writing it right or wrong. Because I really don't know . . . what where exactly how . . . the grammatical rules work out.
> Int.: Do you correct yourself when you talk?
> V: Yeah, I watch out for that very good.
> Int.: How do you know you made a mistake?
> V: . . . it doesn't sound right . . . sometimes what I said I feel it that it doesn't register the way I want it.
> Int.: Do you think grammar rules are useful?
> V: Useful? Yeah. When you want to write they are very very useful.
> Int.: But you don't use them when you write.
> V: Yeah, I know. I don't use them . . . I don't know how to use them!

Another case described by Stafford and Covitt is I, an Israeli woman who has studied English formally and who also values conscious rules highly but utilizes them very little in performance. She is described as being "very friendly . . . loves to talk to people, and is not embarrassed to make mistakes". This outgoing, uninhibited personality type seems to be shared by V, discussed above, and is in contrast to the self-conscious, introverted personality of the overuser. I remarks that even in written performance "first of all I listen to myself as it sounds.

I mean I write it and then I see if it sounds correct." Also, "I listen to things, I don't know the rules. Really, I don't know them." On the other hand, she feels that conscious rules are necessary to speak "correctly". Interestingly, however, she advises a nonrule approach to second language study: "I think when you are a foreigner in a country and you need the language just to speak it daily, you need an audio-visual course, and not, not grammar."

While students like I and V may not directly profit from a rule-type approach to second language, they think they will, and this fact may be a factor in lesson planning.

Conclusion and Summary

Table 1 summarizes the sorts of individual variation discussed here. While this certainly is not an exhaustive listing of every kind of variation seen in adult second language classrooms, it may cover some common types.

Table 1. *Individual variation in Monitor use*

Monitor user	Spoken style	Uses conscious rules?	Personality type
Optimal	−Hesitant	Yes	
Overuser	+Hesitant	Yes	Self-conscious
Underuser	−Hesitant	No*	Outgoing

*May pay lip service to value of rules (see text).

2. Attitude and Aptitude in Second Language Acquisition and Learning

Another area of second language research and practice that the acquisition–learning hypothesis helps to interpret is work in second language *aptitude* and *attitude*, providing a parsimonious explanation for what had appeared to be a strange finding: both language aptitude (as measured by standard tests) and attitude (affective variables) appear to be related to second language achievement, but are not related to each other. It is possible to have high aptitude and low attitude, low aptitude and high attitude, or both high, or both low. In this section, we survey research in these two areas, focusing specifically on the hypothesis that much of what is termed aptitude is directly related to conscious learning, while attitudinal factors may be more closely linked to acquisition.

Aptitude

Foreign language aptitude, which Carroll (1973) defines as the "*rate* at which persons at the secondary school, university and adult level learn to criterion" (p. 5), has most recently been measured by standardized tests such as the *Modern Language Aptitude Test* (MLAT) and the *Language Aptitude Battery* (LAB). According to Carroll (1973), there are three major components of modern aptitude tests. The first, phonetic coding ability, is the ability to store new language sounds in memory. This component will not be of concern to us here. The other two components appear to relate directly to learning.

Grammatical sensitivity, the second component, is defined as "the individual's ability to demonstrate his awareness of the syntactical patterning of sentences in a language" (Carroll, 1973, p. 7). Carroll makes it clear that although performance on this component does not require the subject's actually knowing grammatical terminology, it does involve a conscious meta-awareness of grammar. Carroll contrasts this sort of knowledge of a language with the subconscious or tacit knowledge entailed in Chomsky's term "competence":

> Although it is often said that linguistic "competence" in the sense defined by Chomsky (1965) involves some kind of "knowledge" of the grammatical rules of a language, this "knowledge" is ordinarily out of conscious awareness . . . nevertheless, some adolescents and adults (and even some children) can be made to demonstrate an awareness of the syntactical structure of the sentences they speak . . . even among adults there are large individual differences in this ability, and these individual differences are related to success in learning foreign languages, apparently because this ability is called upon when the student tries to learn grammatical rules and apply them in constructing and comprehending new sentences in that language (pp. 7–8).

Grammatical sensitivity is tapped by the *Words in Sentences* subtest of the Carroll–Sapon MLAT, which asks the testee to pick out the words or phrases in one sentence that "does the same thing" in that sentence as a capitalized word in another sentence. Here is a famous example:

1. He spoke VERY well of you.
2. *Suddenly the* music became *quite loud*.
     1   2   3   4

Most readers will see that the correct answer is "3".

The *Words in Sentences* subtest, like aptitude tests that were developed before the MLAT (reviewed in Carroll, 1963), appears to be related to "general intelligence", as reported by Carroll (1963). Gardner and Lambert (1965, 1972) noted that *Words in Sentences* related not only to achievement in French as a foreign language ("school French achievement", as we shall see below) but also to grades in general and academic achievement outside the foreign language class.

A third component of aptitude is labelled "inductive ability". This is the ability to "examine language material . . . and from this to notice and identify patterns and correspondences and relationships involving either meaning or grammatical form" (Carroll, 1973, p. 8).

"A typical method of measuring this ability is to present materials in an artificial language in such a way that the individual can induce the grammatical and semantic rules governing that language" (Carroll,

1973, p. 8). Carroll also suggests that it is probably through this factor "that foreign language aptitude is most closely related with general intelligence" (p. 8).

Inductive ability also appears to be conscious learning, in that its goal is the discovery of an explicit, abstract (set of) rule(s) by means of a problem-solving approach. The linguist uses the same process in writing a grammar from a corpus.

Pimsleur's summary of the components of language aptitude is quite similar to, but not identical with, Carroll's:

> . . . the "talent" for learning foreign language consists of three components. The first is verbal intelligence, by which is meant both familiarity with words (this is measured in the *Language Aptitude Battery* by the "Vocabulary" part) and the ability to reason analytically about verbal materials (this is measured by the part called "Language Analysis"). The second component is motivation to learn the language. . . . The third component . . . is called "auditory ability" . . . (Pimsleur, 1966, p. 182).

Thus, two of Carroll's components, inductive ability and grammatical sensitivity, and one of Pimsleur's components, verbal intelligence, are hypothesized to relate directly to, or reflect, conscious language learning, the Monitor. The other parts of the aptitude batteries, in both cases, deal with auditory factors (which are not discussed here), and Pimsleur's motivation component forms an additional part of the LAB.

Attitudinal factors that relate to second language acquisition will be those that perform one or both of two functions. First, they will be factors that *encourage intake*. Others have said this before, for example: "motivational variables . . . determine whether or not the student avails himself of . . . informal language contexts" (Gardner, Smythe, Clement, and Gliksman, 1976, p. 200) (see also Oller's Hypothesis 6 in Oller, 1977). They are simply factors that encourage acquirers to communicate with speakers of the target language, and thereby obtain the necessary input, or intake, for language acquisition.

Second, attitudinal factors relating to acquisition will be those that enable the performer to utilize the language heard for acquisition. Simply hearing a second language with understanding appears to be necessary but is not sufficient for acquisition to take place. The acquirer must not only understand the input but must also, in a sense, be "open" to it. Dulay and Burt (1977) have captured this concept by positing the presence of a "socio-affective filter". Performers with high or strong filters will acquire less of the language directed at them, as less input is "allowed in" to the language–acquisition device. The presence of such a filter, according to Dulay and Burt, may explain which of alternative models the acquirer will internalize (e.g. why children acquire the dialect of their peers rather than that of their elders), why acquisition prematurely ceases in some cases, and often what parts of language are acquired first. Thus, attitudinal factors relating to language acquisition will be those that contribute to a *low affective filter*.[1]

The following summary of attitudinal factors will attempt to relate posited predictors of second language proficiency to these two functions.

Integrative motivation, defined as the desire to be like valued members of the community that speak the second language, is predicted to relate to proficiency in terms of the two functions. The presence of integrative motivation should encourage the acquirer to interact with speakers of the second language out of sheer interest, and thereby obtain intake. A low filter for integratively motivated acquirers is also predicted for similar reasons. In Stevick's terms (Stevick, 1976), the integratively motivated performer will not feel a threat from the "other" group (p. 113) and will thus be more prone to engage in "receptive learning" (acquisition), rather than "defensive learning".

Instrumental motivation, defined as the desire to achieve proficiency in a language for utilitarian, or practical reasons, may also relate to proficiency. Its presence will encourage performers to interact with L2 speakers in order to achieve certain ends. For the integratively motivated performer, interaction for its own sake will be valued. For the instrumentally motivated performer, interaction always has some practical purpose.

While the presence of integrative motivation predicts a low affective filter, the presence of instrumental motivation predicts a stronger one. With instrumental motivation, language acquisition may cease as soon as enough is acquired to get the job done. Also, instrumentally motivated performers may acquire just those aspects of the target language that are necessary; at an elementary level, this may be simple routines and patterns, and at a more advanced level this predicts the non-acquisition of elements that are communicatively less important but that are socially important, such as aspects of morphology and accent.[2]

When the practical value of second language proficiency is high, and frequent use necessary, instrumental motivation may be a powerful predictor of second language acquisition.

Personality factors are interrelated with motivational factors. Briefly, it is hypothesized that the self-confident or secure person will be more able to encourage intake and will also have a lower filter. Traits relating to *self-confidence* (lack of anxiety, outgoing personality, self-esteem)[3] are thus predicted to relate to second language acquisition. H. D. Brown (1977) states a similar view: "Presumably, the person with high self-esteem is able to reach out beyond himself more freely, to be less inhibited, and because of his ego strength, to make the necessary mistakes involved in language learning with less threat to his ego" (p. 352). The less self-confident person may understand the input but not acquire, just as the self-conscious person may filter (or avoid) in other domains.

Empathy, the ability to put oneself in another's shoes, is also predicted to be relevant to acquisition in that the empathic person may be the one who is able to identify more easily with speakers of a target language and thus accept their input as intake for language acquisition (lowered affective filter). Empathy appears to interact with other attitudinal factors. Schumann (1975) suggests that ". . . the natural factors that induce ego flexibility and lower inhibitions (assumed to relate to increased empathy) are those conditions which make the learner less anxious, make him feel accepted and make him form positive identifications with speakers of the target language" (p. 227).

Two other personality factors, not related to self-confidence, are also predicted to relate to success in second language. *Attitude toward the classroom and teacher* may relate to both acquisition and learning. The student who feels at ease in the classroom and likes the teacher may seek out intake by volunteering (he may be a "high input generator"; Seliger, 1977), and may be more accepting of the teacher as a source of intake (for exceptionally clear discussion of this point, see Stevick, 1976, chapters 6–8). Positive attitudes toward the classroom and teacher may also be manifestations of self-confidence and/or integrative motivation, and for this reason may also relate to acquisition. In addition, we would expect students with such attitudes to apply themselves more, resulting in more learning.

In addition, students who have an *analytic orientation* should do better in conscious language learning. Subjects who report themselves as more "analytic" or who show test behavior reflecting an analytic cognitive style (e.g. field independent) should do better in conscious learning, and might show a better attitude toward a more analytically oriented classroom, resulting in more acquisition (see above).[3]

Empirical Studies of Aptitude and Attitude

If aspects of aptitude relate directly to conscious language learning, while attitudinal factors generally relate to subconscious language acquisition, certain predictions should hold true. Below we examine these predictions and the supporting evidence.

Prediction no. 1. Attitude and aptitude will be statistically independent, as they relate to very different and independent parts of the language performance and internalization model. Of course, this is a well-established result. Carroll (1963) reported that aptitude is not related to whether or not a person "likes foreign language study" (p. 115), and Gardner and Lambert have confirmed and replicated this result using standard aptitude tests and measures of integrative motivation many times (Gardner, 1960; Gardner and Lambert, 1959, 1972).

Prediction no. 2. The aptitude factor will show a strong relationship to second language proficiency in "monitored" test situations and when conscious learning has been stressed in the classroom. Several studies support this. First, the validity of aptitude tests is usually determined by correlating scores with grades in foreign language classes and/or with pencil and paper grammar tests (Pimsleur, 1966; Carroll, 1963). Such correlations are occasionally, but not always, quite high. Similarly, Gardner (1960) concludes that "language aptitude appears to be of major importance in the acquisition of second language skills acquired through instruction" (p. 214). In his study, three subtests of Carroll's Psi–Lambda aptitude test (Words in

Sentences, Paired Associates, and Spelling Clues) related to several "school-type" tests of French as a foreign language (reading, vocabulary, grammar, pronunciation accuracy, and phonetic discrimination). Gardner and Lambert (1959) presented evidence that "school French achievement", represented by grades in French as well as overall grades, is strongly related to performance on the Words in Sentences subtest of the MLAT, "suggesting that the student who is aware of grammatical distinctions in English will do well in French courses where the emphasis is on grammar" (p. 290). Gardner and Lambert also found a "linguistic reasoning factor": scores on the MLAT related to achievement in reading French, a French grammar test, and a test of phonetic discrimination. While these studies were carried out in Canadian English-speaking situations (Montreal), Gardner and Lambert's subsequent research in the United States (Gardner and Lambert, 1972) confirms these findings.

Gardner, Smythe, Clement, and Gliksman (1976) also confirmed that aptitude related much more to classroom skills (grades) than to communicative skills (speech) in French as a foreign language in grades 7 to 11 in various English-speaking communities in Canada. The effects of aptitude on performance in general was stronger for older students, a finding we shall return to later.

Also of interest is Bialystok and Fröhlich (1977), who studied ninth- and tenth-graders studying French in Toronto. In one or two schools examined, aptitude correlated with self-reports of conscious monitoring ($r = 0.55$).

Finally, recall that Carroll defined aptitude as *rate* of learning, that is, students with higher aptitude will appear to learn faster than students with lower aptitude. This predicts that aptitude will show its strongest effects in a short, well-taught course (Carroll, 1963). Note in this regard that conscious learning may provide a short-cut to performance in a second language. As mentioned elsewhere (Krashen, 1978b; Krashen, 1977a), "learners" can use an acquisition-free mode of performance consisting of first language surface structure plus the Monitor. High-aptitude students should be more likely to be able to utilize this mode and thus may show more rapid initial progress. Over the long term, however, subconscious language acquisition is far superior, as the user of L1 surface structure plus the Monitor is severely limited in terms of the range of structures that can be produced as well as in fluency of performance.

Prediction no. 3. The relationship between attitude and proficiency in second language will be strongest when (a) subjects or performers have had sufficient intake for acquisition (see also Oller, 1977, Hypothesis 6) and (b) when Monitor-free measures of proficiency are used. (Note that attitude will also relate to proficiency when tests that invite the Monitor are used; here both aptitude and attitude will predict proficiency. The effects of attitude will be weaker in this situation, however. Attitudinal effects are predicted to be present whenever any acquired competence at all is used in performance.) Below we review the evidence for each attitudinal factor with respect to this prediction.

Integrative motivation. First, integrative motivation has been found to relate to second language proficiency in situations where intake is available, in the Canadian Anglophone situation, and in the ESL situation in the United States. To briefly review the Canadian situation, Gardner and Lambert (1959), using seventy-five eleventh-grade high school students in Montreal, found integrative motivation to be a stronger predictor of French achievement than instrumental motivation. Gardner (1960) expanded these results with eighty-three tenth-grade students of French. Moreover, he concluded that the integrative motivation was especially important "for the development of communicative skills" (p. 215), while aptitude was important "in the acquisition of second language skills acquired through direct instruction" (p. 214; see discussion above). In a similar setting, Gardner, Smythe, Clement, and Gliksman (1976) confirmed the importance of integrative motivation in grades 7 to 11 French classes in Montreal. They found that measures of integrative motivation tended to correlate more highly with their "speech" measure than with grades. Also, integrative motivation was a better predictor of French proficiency than was instrumental motivation.

Gardner *et al.* also studied factors related to "dropping out" of French (not a compulsory subject in the schools they studied). From their analysis they concluded that those who dropped French were not simply the less "able" students. While drop-outs did tend to get lower grades and show lower aptitude, the primary motivation for the stay-ins appeared to be integrative: stay-ins showed more integrative motivation, as well as overall motivation to learn French. Gardner *et al.* suggest that integrative motivation "provides the student with the necessary motivation to persist in the second language studies" (p. 200).

Integrative motivation also affects actual behavior in the classroom. Gardner *et al.* found that those students whose test responses indicated the presence of integrative motivation volunteered to answer questions more often, made more correct answers in class, and received more positive reinforcement from their teacher. They were also perceived by observers to be more "interested" in the French lesson.

Finally, Bialystok and Fröhlich (1977) reported that measures of integrative motivation correlated with achievement in a test of reading comprehension for ninth- and tenth-grade students of French in Toronto. This study also reported a positive and significant correlation between integrative motivation and aptitude, which is counter to prediction no. 1. To my knowledge, this result has not been reported elsewhere.

As mentioned above, integrative motivation has also been found to relate to proficiency in English as a second language in the United States, another situation in which intake is available outside the classroom. In this case, however, "indirect" methods of measuring integrative motivation have been shown to be necessary. Spolsky (1969) defined integrative motivation as the amount of agreement between a subject's view of himself and his view of speakers of the target language on a variety of personality traits (e.g. stubborn, lazy, kind). This indirect means of determining integrative motivation has been successful, in that measures using this technique with ESL students show clear positive correlations with English proficiency, while direct questionnaires, such as those used in the Canadian studies,[4] did not show such relationships when used with ESL students. Spolsky suggests that foreign students may not want to "admit to motives which suggest they wish to leave their own country permanently" (p. 409).

In another American study, Oller, Hudson, and Liu (1977) studied educated Chinese-speaking ESL students. While these students cited instrumental reasons as primary for studying English, Oller *et al.* found that those subjects who rated Americans as "helpful, sincere, kind, reasonable, and friendly" did better on a Cloze test of English as a second language.

The effect of integrative motivation appears to be weaker in other situations. These situations include those where opportunities to get intake outside the classroom are rare, such as foreign-language learning in the United States. Gardner and Lambert (1972) investigated high-school learning of French in three American communities in Maine, Connecticut, and Louisiana, and only a weak relationship was found in Connecticut.

Also, Oller and colleagues (reported in Oller, 1977) studied the acquisition of English in Japan (English as a foreign language, or EFL), and found little relationship between attitude and proficiency (see also the more recent Chihara and Oller, 1978).

Instrumental motivation may take precedence as a predictor of achievement where there is a special urgency about second language acquisition and where there appears to be little desire to "integrate". As mentioned earlier, instrumental motivation could mean a great deal of interaction in such situations, entailing more intake. The presence of a higher affective filter, however, would predict less success in the long run, however. Two important studies show instrumental motivation to be superior in such situations: Lukmani (1972) found that for female Marathi speakers in Bombay "who belonged to the comparatively non-Westernized section of Bombay society" proficiency in English, as measured by a Cloze test, was more related to instrumental motivation than to integrative. Lukmani concluded that her subjects saw themselves "based in their own country but reaching out to modern ideas and life styles" (p. 272). Gardner and Lambert (1972) reached similar conclusions for English as a second language in the Philippines. In the Philippines English is the language of education and business, but is rarely spoken in the home. Gardner and Lambert found that instrumental motivation was a better predictor of overall English proficiency, but also found a clear relationship between the presence of integrative motivation and "aural–oral" skills, supporting part (b) of this prediction.

Oller, Baca, and Vigil (1977) report on a case where integrative motivation played no role because of political ill-feelings. Sixty Mexican-American females were surveyed in New Mexico, all from low-income families. The subjects who were more proficient in English (a Cloze test was used) tended to rate Americans lower on certain personality traits that are valued by the subjects (religious, sensitive, shy, considerate). Oller *et al.* suggest that these people "feel the oppressive weight of having been absorbed into a powerful political system in which they have traditionally had little power of choice" (p. 182).

Below we review personality factors in relation to prediction no. 3, beginning with those factors relating to self-confidence. Recall that these factors are predicted to be strongest in intake-rich situations, and will emerge most clearly in Monitor-free tests, but will be present to at least some extent when subconscious acquisition is involved.

Anxiety. There appears to be a consistent relationship between various forms of anxiety and language proficiency in all situations, formal and informal. Anxiety level may thus be a very potent influence on the affective filter. These studies have shown a relationship between low anxiety and language acquisition: Carroll (1963) noted a small negative correlation ($r = -0.20$, $n = 68$) between test anxiety and accomplishment in intensive foreign language courses. Gardner, Smythe, Clement, and Gliksman (1976) reported that classroom anxiety correlated with speech skills as well as grades in French as a foreign language in grades 7 to 11 in Canada. There was a trend for low anxiety to be more closely related to speech (Monitor-free) tests than to grades. Naimon, Fröhlich, Stern, and Todesco (1978) found that for their subjects (French students in grades 8 to 12 in Toronto) classroom anxiety, a high fear of rejection and similar feelings may be related to failure. Also, a composite variable consisting of certainty in hand-raising, reaction to being called on without hand-raising, and embarrassment in speaking French, called "overall classroom personality" related to achievement on an imitation test ($r = 0.361$, $p < 0.01$) as well as listening comprehension ($r = 0.380$, $p < 0.01$). Wittenborn, Larsen, and Vigil (1945; reported in Pimsleur, Mosberg, and Morrison, 1962) studied college French and Spanish students, and found that low and high achievers may be distinguished by level of anxiety as well as a degree of self-confidence. Dunkel (1947; also cited in Pimsleur *et al.*, 1962) found that low achievers in Latin showed "emotionality, inner conflict, and anxiety" on a personality test. Oller, Baca, and Vigil (1977), in their study of Mexican-American females in New Mexico, reported that the more subjects saw themselves as "calm, conservative, religious, shy, humble, sincere", the better they did on a Cloze test of English as a second language.

Chastain (1975) reported a significant correlation between test anxiety and success in audio-lingually taught French in an American university. The correlation was negative ($r = -0.48$), indicating that low test anxiety was associated with greater success, which is consistent with the studies cited above. A positive correlation, however, was found between test anxiety and achievement in Spanish (0.21) and German (0.37) taught by "traditional" methods. Anxiety as measured by the Taylor Manifest Anxiety scale was positively correlated with Spanish achievement but showed no other significant relationships. One interpretation of the test anxiety result is that the audio-lingual method actually emphasizes subconscious acquisition, despite its announced intention to establish habits, while "traditional" methods focus on conscious learning. Perhaps low anxiety benefits acquisition, while at least a moderate degree of anxiety may be helpful for learning.

Self-image. Self-image has been shown to be related to second language achievement in a few studies. Heyde (1977) examined the relationship between self-esteem and oral production in ESL performers at the University of Michigan. In her pilot study involving fifteen subjects, she found a high correlation between global self-esteem and teacher ratings of oral production (global self-esteem is defined as the individual's evaluation of his own worth). Oller, Hudson, and Liu (1977), in their study of Chinese-speaking ESL students in the US, found that a variety of positive self-perceptions relate to performance on the Cloze test. Subjects who saw themselves as "democratic, broad-minded, and calm" tended to do better on the Cloze ($r = 0.36$), as did those who saw themselves as "kind, friendly, not business-like, considerate, and helpful" ($r = 0.34$). Since these traits were found to be positively valued by the subjects, Oller *et al.* conclude that "the more positive a subject's self-concept, the higher the subject's achievement in ESL" (p. 14). Also, Naimon, Fröhlich, Stern, and Todesco

(1977), after interviewing teachers as to their views of good and bad language learners, reported that teachers felt that poor learners in the classroom lacked "self-confidence".

Outgoing personality. Outgoing personality may also fit the requirements of prediction no. 3 to some extent. Chastain (1975) reported that performance in foreign language at the college level was related to scores on the Marlowe–Crowne Scale of reserved versus outgoing personality, with outgoing students tending to get higher grades. Pritchard (1952; cited in Pimsleur *et al.*, 1962) observed the playground behavior of thirty-two grammar school boys and found "a correlation of 0.72 between his measures of 'sociability' and the capacity to speak fluently in French" (Pimsleur *et al.*, p. 168). Wesche (1977), studying thirty-seven Canadian civil servants in an intensive French course, found a correlation between "role playing" and proficiency in listening comprehension and speaking skills $(r = 0.60)$. "Role-playing" referred to the willingness of the student to take the part of a character in a dialogue or role-playing situation, "with speech characterized by prosodic expressions of feeling appropriate to the context and by accompanying gestures and facial expressions" (p. 359). This could reflect extroversion, self-confidence, and/or satisfaction with the learning situation, as well as general anxiety level.

Naimon, Fröhlich, Stern, and Todesco (1978) did not find a relationship between proficiency and introversion/extroversion, as measured by the Maudsley Personality Inventory. Naimon *et al.* doubted the validity of this measure in relation to the classroom situation, however: "Often, students who had reported that they were shy and embarrassed, and that they were afraid to speak out in class and were afraid of people laughing at them, and similarly, whom the investigators regarded as being introverted on the basis of classroom observation, scored no differently on many occasions on the Extroversion scale than did students who reported being 'extroverted' and acted accordingly" (p. 261).

Empathy. The evidence here is not overwhelming. Naimon, Fröhlich, Stern, and Todesco (1978) used Hogan's measure of empathy, but found no significant relationship with either listening comprehension or imitation $(r = 0.025$ and $0.008)$ for their students of French as a second language in Toronto high schools. Guiora and his associates have also investigated empathy and second language acquisition in a series of studies with rather variable results. Their pilot study (Guiora, Lane, and Bosworth, 1967) found a 0.60 rank order correlation between French pronunciation accuracy and scores on the Micro-Momentary Expression Device (MME) for fourteen French teachers. Subjects were asked to detect changes in facial expressions and press a button with every perceived change; this was thought to be a reflection of empathy. Subsequent studies did not clearly support the hypothesis that empathy, as measured by the MME, is related to second language pronunciation accuracy. Taylor, Guiora, Catford, and Lane (1970) found that MME performance correlated negatively with pronunciation scores based on a dialogue after a short course in Japanese (28 college students served as subjects). There was a positive correlation between oral production and performance on the TAT Sensitivity to Feelings test. Taylor *et al.* comment as follows: "An interpretation of this result suggests that those individuals who are more aware of feelings are more sensitive to the details and specific aspects of the second language and reflect this in speaking" (p. 154).

In a third study, 401 Defense Language Institute students studying a variety of languages were given the MME and other tests. MME scores did correlate with pronunciation scores for several languages (Spanish, Russian, and Japanese), but a negative correlation was found for Thai and Chinese. Guiora, Brannon, and Dull (1972) suggest that this result may have been due to small sample size for these languages (Thai and Chinese).

Commenting on this series of studies, Schumann (1975) suggests: ". . . we must conclude that neither Taylor *et al.* nor Guiora *et al.* establish that MME is a valid measure of empathy, and that neither study makes it unquestionably clear that MME (and hence empathy) is positively related to authentic pronunciation of a second language" (p. 222). But Schumann continues to say that while "Guiora's theoretical speculations lack experimental verification . . . they do carry intuitive appeal" (p. 224).

The Alcohol Study (Guiora, Beit-Hallahmi, Brannon, Dull, and Scovel, 1972) is perhaps the most suggestive of this group. It was found that pronunciation of Thai sentences was best after 1 to 1¼ ounces of alcohol (but not on an empty stomach). More or less alcohol did not produce the same results. The experimenters suggest that alcohol induced "a flexible psychic state" (p. 52, Guiora, Paluszny, Beit-Hallahmi, Catford, Cooley, and Dull, 1975), with temporary lower inhibitions and presumably heightened empathy. There thus may be "an early positive stage of intoxication" for optimal second language pronunciation, but not for other tasks: there was a trend for performance on a digit-symbol task to get worse with more alcohol. Guiora *et al.* (1972) warn that this positive stage "is very quickly passed. . . . In short, the Alcohol Study made an important theoretical point but has obviously no practical implications for language teaching" (p. 53).

We turn now to factors less directed related to self-confidence.

Attitude toward the classroom and teacher. This factor may relate to both acquisition and learning. Naimon *et al.*, in their study of French as a second language in Toronto, reported that the students' "general attitude" was the best predictor of success: this measure can best be described as an indication of how a student perceives his individual language situation and his general attitude toward learning the language in this particular situation. Data on general attitude were gathered by interviewing the students directly. The experimenter rated the student's general attitude on a five-point scale. This measure of comfort in the class and with the teacher correlated significantly with both an oral test of French (imitation; $r = 0.418$, $p < 0.01$) and a test of listening comprehension ($r = 0.482$, $p < 0.01$). In another study dealing with French in Toronto, Bialystok and Fröhlich (1977) reported that "evaluation of the learning situation" was a good predictor of reading comprehension (along with integrative motivation and motivational intensity) among ninth- and tenth-graders. Gardner *et al.* (1976) found that "evaluative reactions to the learning situation" were associated with both "speech" and grades in levels 7 and 11 in French as a second language in Canada. The relationship with grades tended to be higher than with speech, suggesting that this attitude is related to learning as well as to acquisition.

The analytic personality. Oller, Hudson, and Liu (1977) reported that Chinese ESL acquirers in the United States who viewed themselves as (a) "logical, stubborn, happy", (b) "teachable, friendly", and (c) "clever, broad-minded, intellectual, and calm" tended to do better on a Cloze test of English as a second language. Similarly, Oller, Baca, and Vigil (1977) found that Mexican-Americans who viewed themselves as "logical, sensitive, shy" also tended to do better on a Cloze test of ESL. As discussed above, this factor probably relates more to learning than to acquisition.[3]

Researchers have also attempted to relate field independence and field dependence to second language proficiency, with some degree of success. The field-independent person is better able to perceive parts of a field as distinct from the ground. This ability is thought to be associated with a more analytic ("left-brained") cognitive style. The field-dependent person perceives all parts of the organized field as a total experience (Naimon *et al.*). Field dependence is also associated with the empathic and open personality. There may be a relationship between field independence and second language proficiency in older students; this is supported by Naimon *et al.* for grade 12. It does not appear to relate to proficiency in younger students, however (grades 7 to 11; Naimon *et al.*, 1977; Bialystok and Fröhlich, 1977). Seliger's "high-input generators" (Seliger, 1977), college level ESL students in the US who interacted more in the classroom, tended to be more field independent. Also, Tucker, Hamayan, and Genesee (1976) reported some relationship between field independence and performance on an overall test of French in grade 7, but did not find any relationship with other, more "Monitor-free" tests. The relationship between field independence with older performers (see discussion of child–adult differences below), and with more monitored tests, and the suggested "analytic" cognitive style, implies a relationship between field independence and learning. H. D. Brown (1977) makes just this suggestion, noting that field dependents will tend to be acquirers: "With his empathy and social outreach (the field dependent person) will be a more effective and motivated communicator" (p. 350).

Attitude, Aptitude, and Child–Adult Differences

Monitor Theory, and its proposed interrelationships with aptitude and attitude, allows a clearer picture of the cause of child–adult differences in second language attainment. I have suggested elsewhere (Krashen, 1975a) that the source of the Monitor is *formal operations*, a stage many people, but not all, reach at about age 12 (Inhelder and Piaget, 1958). The formal thinker has the ability to "verbally . . . manipulate relationships between ideas in the absence of prior or concurrent empirical propositions" (Ausubel and Ausubel, 1971, p. 63). For formal thinkers, new concepts are acquired primarily "from verbal rather than from concrete experiences" (*ibid.*, p. 66). The formal thinker also has a meta-awareness of his ideas and can use abstract *rules* to solve a whole class of problems at one time. It is thus plausible that the ability to use a conscious grammar, requiring a meta-awareness of language and general abstract rules, comes as a result of formal operations. (That is to say that formal operations gives the adult a greater ability to make conscious generalizations about language. It is not to say that children, especially older children, have no such ability. They clearly do (Hatch, 1976; Cazden, 1975) but not to as great an extent.) Thus, formal operations may give us the Monitor. But it also has negative effects on language acquisition, a poor exchange that may be the cause of child–adult differences.

According to Elkind (1970), formal operations may have profound affective consequences. I have reviewed Elkind's argument in detail elsewhere (1975b), so I will be brief here. Elkind claims that with formal operations the adolescent gains a greater capacity to conceptualize the thoughts of others. This capacity, however, "is the crux of adolescent egocentrism . . . (the adolescent) fails to differentiate between the objects toward which the thoughts of others are directed and those which are the focus of his own concern" (p. 67). In other words, the adolescent makes the error of thinking that others are thinking about what he is most concerned with: himself. This belief "that others are preoccupied with his appearance and behavior" (p. 53) leads to the increased self-consciousness, feelings of vulnerability, and lowered self-image that are associated with this age. In our terms, it leads to an increased affective filter and a subsequently lowered ability to acquire a second language. (Pronunciation seems to be the most difficult aspect of a second language to acquire after this age, perhaps because it runs "deeper into the center of the student's personality than any other aspect of language" (Stevick, 1976, p. 64; see also Seliger, Krashen, and Ladefoged, 1975).

This hypothesis has its predictions as well.

Prediction no. 1. Aptitude, since it relates directly to conscious language learning, or the Monitor, will not be a strong predictor of second language success in children acquiring a second language. This prediction has been confirmed. Tucker, Hamayan, and Genesee (1976) gave three groups of grade 7 students of French attitude and aptitude tests. For all subjects, measures of attitude and motivation related to achievement in French and were much better predictors than aptitude and IQ measures. The strongest predictors were a positive attitude toward the target language and high need achievement. Gardner *et al.* (1976) report data that also support this prediction. In grade 7 French as a second language, aptitude was found to be less important as a predictor of French achievement than in later grades.

Prediction no. 2. Attitudinal factors will predict second language achievement for children whenever intake is available. There has been little work in this area. Fillmore (1976), in her case study of five children acquiring English as a second language in an American kindergarten, does provide some clear evidence. Nora, Fillmore's most successful acquirer, "was strongly motivated to be associated with English-speaking children . . . she sought them out to play with to an extent that none of the other children in the study did" (p. 706). This may be interpreted as integrative motivation. Nora also exhibited self-confidence in her approach to language acquisition: "in contrast (to some of the other children) Nora was quite uninhibited in her attempts at speaking the new language . . . from the first she was more concerned with communication than form" (p. 710). Hatch (1976) has also documented cases from diary studies where affective and attitudinal factors played a role in success of child second language acquisition.

Using a more experimental approach, Swain and Burnaby (1976) studied affective variables in the "immersion" kindergarten. Successful acquisition of French by English-speaking children showed some relationship to "perfectionism" as well as level of anxiety. Other measures, such as "sociability" and "talkativeness", did not show a relationship to French proficiency. Swain and Burnaby point out, however, that such traits are not encouraged in the classroom situation. This helps to explain the difference between these results and those reported by Pritchard (1952; see above).

The Good Language Learner Revisited

If all the above is true, it predicts that above all the "good language learner" is an *acquirer*, who first of all is able to obtain sufficient intake in the second language, and second, has a low affective filter to enable him to utilize this input for language acquisition. The good language learner may or may not be a conscious learner. If he is, he is an "optimal Monitor user". We would therefore not be surprised to see above average or superior language aptitude in such a performer.

Data from Naimon *et al.* (1978) support these generalizations. They surveyed thirty-four "good language learners", and found that *immersion* and *motivation* were the most frequent responses to the question of what factors influenced successful second language acquisition. Further, they reported that "there is some evidence in the interview . . . that those subjects who learned a language in the country of the target language, though frequently combined with self-study, usually acquired it successfully" (p. 34). This conclusion is similar to that reached by Carroll (1967), in his study of college foreign language majors, as well as in other studies (Krashen, 1976a; Chapter 3, this volume).

The Good Language Learners in Naimon *et al.* (1978) agreed that the study of grammar alone was not enough: "Several interviewees, who had achieved high marks in their language courses at school, now attached little significance to this aspect of success" (p. 34).

Thus, the mixture of formal and informal experience with the second language appeared to be the most popular approach. One subject, for example, Mr. "E", while immersing himself in the country where the target language was spoken, would study on his own, a lesson a day in a formal grammar.

Good language learners/acquirers must do more than just be present in informal and formal environments, however. It appears to be the case that they "go out and get" intake and have a low enough filter to utilize it for language acquisition. While many of them consciously learn (12/34 in Naimon *et al.* indicated that conscious rules were useful for them; in Wesche, 1977, 6/11 said the same thing), they appeared to be optimal Monitor users, using learning as a supplement to acquisition in certain conditions.

The Bad Language Learner

There seem to be three sorts of bad language learners. The very worst has neither acquisition nor learning going for him. This might be the result of both attitudinal factors (lack of interest in the target language and its speakers and/or self-consciousness, high anxiety, etc.) as well as low aptitude or interest in grammar. The second language student who seems to get nothing from the class or the natural environment may be of this sort (the "remedial ESL student").

Two other varieties of bad language learners have been discussed elsewhere (Krashen, 1978a; Chapter 1, this volume). The underuser of the Monitor will progress as far as his attitudes will take him. The Monitor overuser will be limited by his conscious knowledge and will suffer from a lack of spontaneity.

The model predicts that all varieties of performers will be helped by a classroom where intake for acquisition is available in a low anxiety situation. This is easy to say but difficult to provide. Conscious learning need not be avoided, just put in its place. This recommendation is quite close to Carroll's: "Persons with limited sensitivity to grammar may be better off in courses that de-emphasize grammar and concentrate on exposing the learner to large amounts of the second language in actual use. Nevertheless, many of them will find it profitable to note carefully, and to try to correct, the errors they make in second language utterances. Others, as they use the language more and more, may find it satisfactory simply to wait until a natural correction process takes over, somewhat the way children learn to speak their native language in increasing conformity with adult norms" (Carroll, 1977, p. 3). We differ only in that the Monitor Theory predicts that the acquisition-rich environment is for everyone.

If, in fact, acquisition is central and obligatory for real proficiency in a second language, and if, at best, learning is a useful supplement available only in certain situations, and if attitude relates more directly to acquisition that to learning, then Savignon (1976) is correct when she says "Attitude is the single most important factor in second language learning". We might even suggest that one characteristic of the ideal second language class is one in which aptitude will *not* predict differences in student achievement (S. Sapon, personal communication), because efficient acquisition is taking place for all students.

Notes

[1] The presence of such a filter may explain why some foreign language students behave like patients with bilateral hippocampal lesions. Stevick (1976) notes that such patients "are perfectly normal in intelligence, and they can remember the words and language skills that they had before the operation. Further, they have no difficulty in hearing, understanding, and repeating new information as long as they keep on repeating it. They are different from other people in only one respect: if their repetition of the new material is interrupted in any way, they forget it immediately ..." (pp. 6–7). Moreover, "the behavior of these patients is embarrassingly similar to the classroom behavior of our students" (p. 7).

[2] We might say that the instrumental acquirer or learner "fossilizes" (Selinker, 1972), or ceases progress when he perceives that communicative needs are met. The integrative acquirer/learner fossilizes when he perceives that his social needs are met.

[3] While attitudinal effects are, it is hypothesized, directly related to acquisition, they may certainly be indirectly related to conscious learning. For example, the integratively motivated student might clearly be willing to spend more time and effort in conscious learning, especially if he has been taught that such an effort is useful. Also, there are conditions under which high aptitude may lead to acquisition, albeit indirectly. The high-aptitude student probably feels drawn toward learning; such learning may have very satisfying results in terms of the rapid sort of progress it seems to give at first. In terms of Monitor Theory, this is not real progress—it may produce "language-like" behavior, achieved by the use of the first language as a substitute utterance initiator with Monitor repairs (the L1 + Monitor mode; Krashen, 1977a). In addition to the affective benefit the use of this mode may have, it may indirectly encourage acquisition by drawing more intake to the performer. Use of this mode may allow the performer some degree of interaction with second language speakers. The use of routines and patterns also does this and may also encourage intake (Fillmore, 1976; Krashen and Scarcella, 1978). (Part of this input may be the pseudo-language of others. The mechanisms used by the speaker in producing someone else's input, of course, make no difference to the hearer, however, and it is legitimate input.)

[4] For example, one attitudinal test used by Gardner and Lambert (1959) asked students to rank four possible reasons for studying French:
Knowledge of French would
1. be useful in obtaining a job,
2. be helpful in understanding the French-Canadian people and their way of life,
3. permit meeting and conversing with more and varied people,
4. make one a better educated person.
A fifth alternative, "any other personal reason", was also permitted. Gardner and Lambert explain that "S's who ranked either alternative (2) or (3) as most relevant were classified as 'integratively oriented'. Those choosing either (1) or (4) were classified as 'instrumentally oriented'. Those choosing alternative (5) were not classified" (p. 193).

3. Formal and Informal Linguistic Environments in Language Acquisition and Language Learning

The question of the optimal linguistic environment for the adult second language student has been approached empirically in the last few years in a number of studies. It is a question of obvious importance to the teacher and language student and has also become a matter of concern to the psycholinguist interested in the nature of primary linguistic data, or linguistic input necessary for language acquisition to occur.

In these studies, two sorts of linguistic environments are contrasted: artificial, or formal environments, found for the most part in the classroom, and natural, or informal environments. Krashen and Seliger (1975) have noted that all language teaching systems utilized for the adult use activities in which linguistic rules are presented one at a time and in which some sort of feedback (error correction and/or error detection) is present. Other features of formal instruction (e.g. deductive presentation of rules) are not common to all teaching methods and, while their presence may sometimes be catalytic, are not necessary for learning to take place. Krashen and Seliger also note that these features (rule isolation and feedback) do not seem to be present in informal environments.

Several studies, which will be considered in some detail below, suggest that adults can not only increase their second language proficiency in informal environments, but may do as well as or better than learners who have spent a comparable amount of time in formal situations. Other studies present evidence that seems to indicate that "exposure" has little or no effect on increasing adult second language proficiency. In the literature review that follows, it will be argued that these studies are not definitive. Even taken as a group, they do not settle the issue of whether adults are able to acquire language in informal situations with any real efficiency. Following the survey, it will be argued that formal and informal environments make contributions to different aspects of second language competence.

We are thus considering two hypotheses:

1. The informal environment can be efficiently utilized by the adult second language learner.
2. Formal study, or its essential characteristics, is significantly more efficient than informal exposure in increasing second language proficiency in adults.

Review of Literature

Upshur (1968) compared three groups of ten adult ESL students enrolled in a special summer session for law students at the University of Michigan. The first group, who scored highest on the entrance test (Michigan Examination in Structure), attended seminars and classes during the 7-week period that were conducted in English, but had no extra ESL classes. The second group, who scored lower on the entrance test, also attended law classes and had 1 hour daily of ESL in addition. The third group scored lowest on the pre-test and had 2 hours of ESL daily in addition to law classes. At the end of the summer, an alternate form of the pre-test was given. While all three groups showed some improvement in performance, Upshur's statistical analysis revealed "no significant effects on language learning attributable to amount of language instruction", and concluded that "foreign language courses may at this time be less effective means for producing language learning than the use of language in other activities". This is a strong version of hypothesis I.

Upshur's conclusion appears to be consistent with his data. Krashen and Seliger (1975) suggest, however, that motivated second language students are able to provide themselves with the essential ingredients of formal instruction without going to class. Rule isolation can be done by recourse to a text or by asking informants about grammar, while feedback is available when helpful friends correct the learner. Without extensive probing of the private lives of those involved in the study, however, this alternative explanation is untestable. Nevertheless, it may be true.

Mason (1971) is also interpretable in these two ways. In this study, certain foreign students at the University of Hawaii were allowed to follow regular academic programs without extra ESL, despite the fact that their English placement scores indicated that they should be enrolled in English for foreign student classes. Post-tests given at the end of the semester showed no significant difference in increase in English proficiency between those excused from ESL and controls who took the required ESL classes. These data are again consistent with hypothesis I, but other explanations are available, including the "self-study" hypothesis described above, which is consistent with hypothesis II.

Carroll (1967) studied the second language proficiency of American college seniors majoring in foreign languages (French, German, Russian, Spanish). About 25 per cent of the total population of senior language majors that year (N = 2784) were given form A of the MLA Foreign Language Proficiency test in their language. Carroll's major finding was that, on the average, foreign language majors performed rather poorly: the median score on the MLA corresponded to a Foreign Service Institute rating of 2 plus (out of 5) (between "limited working proficiency" and "minimum professional proficiency"). Of more interest here is the relation found between attainment* and measures of time spent in different linguistic environments. A strong relationship was found between time spent abroad (in the country where the target language was spoken) and test performance, with those who reported a year's study abroad doing best, followed by those who reported a summer abroad or a tour. Both of these groups outperformed those who had never been in the country where the target language was spoken.

A significant relationship was also found between test performance and the extent to which the target language was used in the students' home. (Native speakers of the language majored in were excluded from the study.) Those reporting frequent parental use of the target

---

* The listening subtest alone was used in this and subsequent analyses, as intercorrelations among subtests was high.

language had higher scores than students who reported occasional use, and this latter group outperformed those whose parents did not or could not speak the target language at home. These two findings (time abroad and parental use) are consistent with hypothesis I but could fit hypothesis II: use of the language at home may have increased motivation to study, and time spent abroad may have meant more formal study and/or more chances for self-study, as well as increased motivation to learn formally.

Hypothesis II also receives independent support from Carroll's study. It was found that those who started foreign language study early (grade school) achieved better scores. Those who studied the target language in high school did better than those who started in college (German majors were an exception to this). This relationship was independent of that found between proficiency and time spent in informal environments. Carroll notes that "the simplest explanation of this finding is that the attainment of skill in a foreign language is a function of the amount of time spent in its study" (p. 136). The following series of studies also argue for hypothesis II.

Krashen and Seliger (1976) and Krashen, Seliger, and Hartnett (1974) claim that when the effects of "exposure" and formal instruction are compared, it is reliably the case that more instruction means higher proficiency, while more exposure does not necessarily mean more proficiency in ESL. Both studies compared instruction and exposure by matching pairs of foreign students for one of these variables and seeing whether the student who excelled on the other was more proficient in English.

The measure of the amount of formal instruction was simply the students' report of the number of years he or she had studied English in a school situation. No questions were asked concerning factors such as the methodology used, the presence or absence of a language laboratory, how often the class met, the amount of time the student devoted to his studies, or grades received. In Krashen and Seliger (1976), exposure was defined as the product of the number of years the student reported having spent in an English-speaking country and how much English the student said he spoke every day (on a scale of 1 to 10). In Krashen *et al.* (1974) students were asked to indicate years spent in an English-speaking country and also to indicate how much

English they spoke each day (on a scale of 1 to 4). Subjects with the same number of years spent in the country where English was spoken and the same report of speaking were considered to have the same exposure score.

Student samples differed somewhat. In Krashen and Seliger, subjects were registered in an intensive, 20 hour per week institute designed to prepare foreign students for study in American colleges. In Krashen *et al.*, subjects were enrolled in a part-time extension program; these students were, on the average, older, and many were permanent residents or citizens of the United States. The measure of proficiency used in the first study was teacher ranking (which correlated significantly with local placement tests), and in the second study the Michigan Examination in Structure was used.

In the first study, six out of fourteen pairs of students matched for years of formal study of English were consistent with the hypothesis that more exposure meant more proficiency; that is, in only six cases did the student with more exposure show a higher ranking than his partner with less. Similarly, in the second study, more exposure was associated with a higher score in only ten out of twenty-one cases, which is consistent with the hypothesis that exposure has no consistent effect on second language proficiency. When students were matched for exposure scores, however, it appeared to be the case that more instruction did indeed mean more proficiency. In the first study, this was true of seven out of nine cases, and in the second it was true of eight out of eleven cases, which in both studies was statistically significant.

Krashen, Jones, Zelinski, and Usprich (1978) arrived at similar results. Placement test scores for 115 students of English as a second language in an extension program were correlated with students' reports of years of formal study and years spent in an English-speaking country. The results (Table 1) confirm the conclusions of the studies described above: years of formal instruction reported is a better predictor of English proficiency than is time spent in an English-speaking environment. While exposure, here simply the report of years spent in an informal environment with no estimation of how much the S used the target language, was shown to have a significant effect, it accounted for relatively little of the variation in test scores.

Table 1. *English proficiency and years in an English-speaking country and years of formal English study*[*]

Test	Correlation with years in an English-speaking country	
	r	p
Michigan (Exam. in structure)	0.18	$p<0.05$
Composition	0.22	$p<0.025$
Cloze	0.24	$p<0.01$
Test	Correlation with reported years of formal ESL study	
	r	p
Michigan (Exam. in structure)	0.50	$p<0.001$
Composition	0.34	$p<0.005$
Cloze	0.47	$p<0.001$

[*] From Krashen, Jones, Zelinski, and Usprich (1978).

Discussion of Literature Survey

The last three studies described above (Krashen and Seliger, 1976; Krashen, Seliger, and Hartnett, 1974; Krashen, Jones, Zelinski, and Usprich, 1978) provide explicit support for hypothesis II. These three studies, however, share a feature that prevents them from being convincing counterexamples to hypothesis I. "Years spent in an English-speaking country" need not be equivalent to time spent in meaningful informal linguistic environment. There is an important difference between the measures used in the Upshur, Mason, and Carroll studies and in the measure used in the Krashen *et al.* series. In the former group of studies, we can be fairly certain that the second language student was involved in real and sustained second language use situations. Upshur and Mason's subjects were university students who were taking courses taught in English. In addition, they were also probably taking part in the social life of their respective schools. Carroll's "year abroad" students were also highly likely to have been engaged in real communicative use of the language, as their primary purpose for going abroad, in most cases, was to have additional opportunities to converse with native speakers of the language they were studying. In the Krashen *et al.* series, we have much less knowledge of just how much or what percentage of time was spent in real and sustained language use. In the first two of the three Krashen *et al.* studies, the exposure measure included a self-rating of how much English the subject spoke each day, but as Krashen and Seliger (1976) point out, this estimate may not have been true of the entire time the S spent in the second language environment: some may have spent a fair amount of time in the United States before attempting to use English regularly. In the third study of this series, only "years in an English-speaking country" was considered. A significant number of subjects who did not use the language regularly may have affected the results for the sample. Thus, the Upshur, Mason, and Carroll subjects appear to have been involved in an intensive, daily, and often demanding second language environment. The Krashen *et al.* subjects may have varied much more with respect to the amount of real communicative use they made of their second language.

While the characteristics of utilized primary linguistic data (termed "intake" in recent years) have not been determined in detail,* mere "heard language" is probably insufficient input for the operation of a language acquisition device at any age. The difference between "heard language" and "intake" is emphasized in Friedlander, Jacobs, Davis, and Wetstone (1972), who examined the linguistic environment of a child who at 22 months was judged to be nearly as fluent in Spanish as she was in English. The child heard Spanish primarily from her father. This input, according to Friedlander *et al.*, made up only 4 per cent of the child's total "heard language" but was 25 per cent of the language directed at the child. This confirms the hypothesis that the relevant primary linguistic data are those which the acquirer is actively involved with: the total linguistic environment is less important.

The results of the studies reviewed here can all be considered as consistent with hypothesis I. The Upshur, Mason, and Carroll studies are direct evidence, while the Krashen *et al.* series may be interpreted as showing that acquisition from the informal environment requires regular and intensive language use. Hypothesis II, however, also receives no counter-evidence from any of the studies. The correlations between years of formal study and proficiency found by Krashen *et al.* are reliable and are consistent with Carroll's interpretation of his data.

---

* See Chapter 9 for further discussion.

The "self-study" reinterpretation of Upshur's and Mason's results, as well as Carroll's "year abroad" and "home use" data, remains a plausible, but difficult to test, explanation.

In the following section, it is proposed that modifications of hypotheses I and II are correct: formal and informal environments contribute to second language competence in different ways or, rather, to different aspects of second language competence. To support this hypothesis, we will reinterpret the literature surveyed here in terms of the acquisition–learning distinction. In addition, we will consider some cross-sectional data that eliminate certain alternative explanations presented in the literature survey and confirm several hypotheses presented above.

Contributions of Formal and Informal Environments

It is not simply the case that informal environments provide the necessary input for *acquisition* while the classroom aids in increasing *learned* competence. The reinterpretation of the Krashen *et al.* series as well as the Friedlander *et al.* data described above suggests, first of all, that informal environments must be intensive and involve the learner directly in order to be effective. One might then distinguish "exposure-type" informal environments and "intake-type" environments. Only the latter provide true input to the language acquisition device. Second, it seems plausible that the classroom can accomplish both learning and acquisition simultaneously. While classwork is directly aimed at increasing conscious linguistic knowledge of the target language, to the extent that the target language is used realistically, to that extent will acquisition occur. In other words, the classroom may serve as an "intake" informal environment as well as a formal linguistic environment.

Both of these points are illustrated and confirmed by new data on proficiency and linguistic environment using the SLOPE test with adult learners of English. The subject pool was the same as used in Krashen, Sferlazza, Feldman, and Fathman (1976): sixty-six subjects were tested, with thirteen first language groups being represented. Some had studied English intensively while others had encountered English only in informal environments. Table 2 shows the relationship between overall SLOPE scores and measures of exposure. Despite our findings that the SLOPE, as administered, is primarily an *acquisition* measure (because it yielded a "natural" difficulty order and allowed no monitoring time), no relationship was found between the measure of exposure and SLOPE scores.

These results confirm the suspicions voiced above about using "exposure-type" measures of informal linguistic environments, and underline the claim that active involvement is necessary for acquisition

Table 2. *SLOPE performance and measures of exposure and formal instruction*

	Years in English-speaking country		Years of formal English study	
	r	p	r	p
SLOPE scores	0.014	ns	0.42	$p < 0.001$

Partial correlations were used, as years in English-speaking country and years of formal study were correlated, $r = -0.24$, $p < 0.01$. Ordinary correlations were computed, however, and were quite similar to those reported above; for SLOPE and exposure, $r = 0.003$, and for SLOPE and formal study, $r = 0.40$.

to take place. Thus, if the SLOPE is a test of acquired competence only, it must be concluded that the question asked in the Krashen *et al.* series is a measure of time spent in "exposure-type" environments only, and this apparent counter-evidence to hypothesis I disappears entirely. No studies in the literature survey, however, are counter-evidence to the hypothesis that an "intake-type" informal environment may be quite efficient in increasing adult second language proficiency.

The significant correlation in Table 2 between years of formal instruction and SLOPE scores supports the hypothesis that the classroom can be of value, and in fact generally *is* of value, in language acquisition as well as in language learning.

While all studies described here are consistent with a revised version of hypothesis II, that in general formal instruction increases second language proficiency, none of the studies gives evidence to indicate that "learning" does indeed take place in formal situation in addition to acquisition. Note that "learning" occurs in the Upshur and Mason studies only under the "self-study" hypothesis, while in the Krashen *et al.* series the evidence for learning is the positive correlation between years of formal study and proficiency. The SLOPE data indicated, however, that the classroom second language experience may also influence the acquired competence, and we thus have no direct evidence that learning takes place at all. The hypothesis that the classroom contributes to acquisition only is sufficient to predict all the data covered above, as all proficiency tests, according to the Monitor Theory, involve some acquired competence.

There is, however, evidence that learning exists, and may increase proficiency. An interesting case of an advanced ESL performer ("P", discussed in Krashen and Pon, 1975, and in Chapter 1, this volume) supports the hypothesis that learning may increase performed accuracy by supplementing the acquired output. Our subject performed nearly perfectly in situations where monitoring was possible, but made errors in casual speech. She could, however, correct nearly all these errors and could also describe the grammatical rules she broke. This suggests that consciously learned competence was involved in those situations in which she made less errors.

Conclusion

The child relies primarily on acquisition. Thus, "intake" informal environments are sufficient. The class can provide only additional intake, and it appears to be the case that when children have access to rich intake environments, extra classes in second languages are not necessary (Fathman, 1975; Hale and Budar, 1970).

The Upshur, Mason, and Carroll studies are consistent with the hypothesis that intake informal environments can be quite beneficial for adult second language acquisition, and the distinction between intake and exposure-type informal environments disallows the Krashen *et al.* series as counterevidence to hypothesis I. The ineffectiveness of exposure type environments is confirmed by the lack of relationship between reports of time spent in the country where the target language was spoken and the results of an "acquisition" proficiency test. No studies provide counterevidence to a modified version of hypothesis II: formal environments are also beneficial. The need to decide between the original formulations of hypotheses I and

II is obviated by an independently justified model of adult second language competence in which intake informal environments and formal instruction make different sorts of contributions to second language competence.

Table 3. *Linguistic environments relevant to second language proficiency in adults*

	In the classroom		Outside the classroom		
	"intake" informal (language use)	formal	"intake" informal	"exposure" informal	formal (self-study)
Acquisition	*		*		
Learning		*			*

Table 3 summarizes the implications of the literature survey and SLOPE data in terms of Monitor Theory. Both formal and informal linguistic environments contribute to second language proficiency but do so in different ways: an intensive intake informal environment can provide both the adult and child with the necessary input for the operation of the language acquisition device. The classroom can contribute in two ways: as a formal linguistic environment, providing rule isolation and feedback for the development of the Monitor, and, to the extent language use is emphasized, simultaneously as a source of primary linguistic data for language acquisition.

4. The Domain of the Conscious Grammar: The Morpheme Studies

The Morpheme Studies: A brief history

The study of grammatical morphemes has been particularly fruitful for understanding the mechanisms involved in second language acquisition by adults. Aside from merely telling us in what order certain structures are in fact acquired, these studies have also been of value in revealing the domain of the acquired and learned grammars, when performers appeal to conscious learning and when they do not.

The history of morpheme studies in language acquisition begins with Brown's demonstration (Brown, 1973) that children acquiring English as a first language show a similar order of acquisition for grammatical morphemes in obligatory occasions. Certain morphemes, such as *ing* and *plural*, tend to be acquired relatively early, while others, such as the third person singular /s/ on verbs in the present tense (III sing.) or the possessive *'s* marker tend to be acquired late. Brown's longitudinal findings were confirmed cross-sectionally by de Villiers and de Villiers (1973). This discovery was extended to child second language acquisition by Dulay and Burt (1973, 1974a, 1975) in several cross-sectional studies, by Kessler and Idar (1977), and by Rosansky (1976) (who has a rather different view of her results, to be discussed below). The child second language order was not identical to the child first language order, but there were clear similarities among second language acquirers. (As I have pointed out in several places (Krashen, 1977a; Krashen, Butler, Birnbaum, and Robertson, 1978), this appears to be due to differences in the rank order of free morphemes, especially copula and auxiliary, which tend to come later for the first language acquirer.)

The discovery of the "natural order" has allowed us to probe the interaction between language acquisition and language learning in the

51

adult performer: we have interpreted the presence of the "natural order" (the child's order of acquisition or difficulty order) in the adult performer as a manifestation of the acquired system without substantial interruption or contribution from the conscious grammar, or Monitor.

As we shall see, our current results dovetail nicely not only with our intuitions about the use of conscious rules but also with speculations and results from other areas of second language acquisition research.

Grammatical morpheme studies with adults began with our (Bailey, Madden, and Krashen, 1974) finding that adult second language acquirers (ESL students at Queens College) showed a "natural order" for eight grammatical morphemes, a difficulty order similar to that found in child second language acquirers by Dulay and Burt, with oral language elicited by the Bilingual Syntax Measure (Burt, Dulay, and Hernandez, 1975). We also reported no difference in rank order between Spanish-speakers and non-Spanish-speakers, which was consistent with Dulay and Burt's finding of no first language influence in their child second language study (Chinese-speakers and Spanish-speakers; Dulay and Burt, 1974a). We also noted that our difficulty order was similar to the order found by de Villiers (1974) for adult agrammatics.

Following our study, Larsen-Freeman (1975) reported a "natural order", again cross-sectionally, for both BSM elicited speech and an imitation task. Her own tests, which included "reading", "writing", and "listening", did not show a natural order, and I speculated (Krashen, 1976a, 1977a) that this was due to the intrusion of the conscious grammar, which caused an elevation in the accuracy of those items that were "easiest" to learn (third person singular morpheme, regular past morpheme). When performance is "Monitor-free" (little time, focus on communication and not form) we thus see the "natural order" for grammatical morphemes, a difficulty order similar to that seen in the child. When performance is "monitored", the natural order is disturbed. The BSM, it was suggested, is such a Monitor-free test, while Larsen-Freeman's pencil and paper "grammar-type" tests invite the use of the Monitor. We return to Larsen-Freeman's results below.

Our study using the SLOPE test, an oral production test designed by

Ann Fathman, confirmed our earlier results. Again, adult performers showed a difficulty order similar to that seen in children acquiring ESL. Again, there was no strong first language influence. Also, there was no difference in rank order between formal learners and informal acquirers, the former groups being those who reported having had a great deal of instruction in English and little real use, and the latter being those who reported a great deal of real world exposure to English but little or no classroom instruction. Our interpretation of this result was that both groups were dependent on the acquired system, since the test did not encourage conscious monitoring (Krashen, Sferlazza, Feldman, and Fathman, 1976).

At about this time, Roger Andersen (1976) reported a "natural order" for adult ESL students in Puerto Rico using compositions. We also undertook a composition study soon after (Krashen, Butler, Birnbaum, and Robertson, 1978): in our study, we asked ESL students to write under two conditions, "fast", in which they were told to write as much as possible in a short time (in the style of Brière's 1966 "Quantity before Quality" study), and "edited", in which they were encouraged to go over their work carefully. We found a natural order in both conditions, with only small evidence of a contribution from the conscious grammar in the edited condition. Our interpretation of these results was that students were concerned with communication when writing rather than with form; apparently the "focus on form" condition for Monitor use discussed earlier (see Introduction) is more crucial for bringing out the Monitor than is the "time" condition: our subjects did indeed have time, but they did not use it for the conscious grammar, for conscious monitoring. This is not to say they did not edit—it does imply that when they do edit, they do not use their conscious knowledge to any great extent when communication is the issue.

A more recent study confirms this, and suggests that it may take a very special kind of task to encourage subjects to use the Monitor. (This is not to say that we feel Monitor use is inherently good. We are interested here in the theoretical question of when people use it and when they do not.) Noel Houck, Judith Robertson, and I have just completed a study in which we asked USC ESL students to transcribe their own speech and then to correct their own transcripts. Both activities show a natural order for grammatical morphemes, despite the fact that at least some of the corrections were aimed at morphology. We were struck by the fact that natural orders, at least in our laboratory, were turning up everywhere, and we replicated one of the few studies that reported to give an unnatural order, Larsen-Freeman's "writing" task. The replication was successful; this task again produced a clearly unnatural order, one that was nearly identical to Larsen-Freeman's reported order. While both tasks seem to imply a focus on form (self-correction and the writing task), there are crucial differences. In their self-corrections, the composition students were not focused on a particular item or on a specific rule, and apparently did the task on the basis of their "feel" for grammaticality. Their corrections were apparently motivated by their desire to communicate. In Larsen-Freeman's writing task, which included sentences like:

Last year he (work) _____ in a factory

where the subject only had to correctly inflect the verb, there might have been a greater tendency to call forth conscious rules for specific items. In other words, Larsen-Freeman's task was what is called a *discrete-point* test, while ours was not. This leads to the interesting hypothesis that it takes a discrete-point test to bring out conscious learning, while anything less does not, at least for subjects who have had a chance to do a meaningful amount of natural acquisition. Thus, we might expect a discrete-point test to yield an unnatural order and an integrative test to yield a natural order. So far this is what we have found. (In a previous paper (Krashen, 1976a) I suggested that integrative tests were not necessarily acquisition tests. In those days, I had only considered the time element as the necessary condition for Monitor use. This was clearly inadequate, and I thank Heidi Dulay and Marina Burt for pointing out that having time is not sufficient to ensure Monitor use, and John Oller for pointing out that my conclusions on integrative testing were premature, suggestions that are certainly confirmed by these current data.)

Janet Keyfetz Fuller's dissertation (Fuller, 1978) also speaks to this point. Fuller administered the SLOPE test to adult ESL subjects in both written and oral versions. She tested the effect of first language (Indo-European versus non-Indo-European), second versus third language acquisition, and order of presentation. In general, there were no significant differences for any of these contrasts. She also found no significant rank order differences between the oral and written versions, despite the fact that performers clearly had more time for the written version. (In Krashen, Sferlazza, Feldman, and Fathman, 1976, we had attempted to run a written version of the SLOPE with our subjects but could not analyze the data due to ceiling effects; we noted a clear rise in III singular rank order, however.) Are Fuller's results consistent with the hypothesis that learning is brought out only by a discrete-point test?

The SLOPE test does ask the subject for an item in a slot, and to that extent it has some of the characteristics of a discrete-point test. A SLOPE item might look like:

> Here is a ball. (Picture)
> Here are two _____ . (Picture)

This differs in a crucial way from the example given above from Larsen-Freeman's test. In the SLOPE the subject contributes the entire item, while for many items in Larsen-Freeman's writing test the subject need only inflect a given form. This may focus the subject more clearly on *form*. Whether this is the crucial difference remains to be seen and can easily be tested.

Also, these results may not hold for foreign language as well as second language performers. Generally, foreign language students have less access to language acquisition and rely more on learning. It would not be at all surprising if foreign language students show a greater learning effect, manifested by more "unnatural orders". Adult EFL students in other countries might provide the crucial data here.

Objections to the "Natural Order"

1. Is the natural order an artifact of the Bilingual Syntax Measure?

There have been some critiques and objections to this seemingly clear and consistent picture. First, several scholars have suggested that the adult natural order is an artifact of the use of the Bilingual Syntax Measure (Porter, 1977; Hakuta and Cancino, 1977; Rosansky, 1976). This suspicion was based on the following circumstantial evidence:

the Dulay and Burt child second language studies used the BSM, the Bailey *et al.* adult study used the BSM, and when Larsen-Freeman used the BSM she obtained a similar order, but when she used other tasks she did not. Also, Porter (1977) reported that child first language acquirers produced what appeared to be the *second* language acquisition order when the BSM was used; as pointed out above, first and second language acquisition orders are somewhat different. While this evidence is at first glance suggestive, recent studies and reanalyses show conclusively, I believe, that the natural order is not an artifact of the BSM. First, we have obtained the natural order without the BSM, in the composition studies cited above, and more recently adult-free (spontaneous) speech (Krashen, Houck, Giunchi, Bode, Birnbaum, and Strei, 1977). Also, the SLOPE test gives an order quite similar to that found in the grammatical morpheme studies (Krashen *et al.*, 1976; Fuller, 1978). (Some of these data were obtained and reported on after this objection was raised.) Second, Porter's child first language BSM order is not at all dissimilar to first language orders previously published in the literature (rho = 0.67 with de Villiers and de Villiers, 1973, which just misses the 0.05 level of significance, quite impressive for a rank order correlation using just seven items). (For a fuller discussion, see my response to Porter (Krashen, 1978c) in *Language Learning.*)

2. Do cross-sectional and longitudinal studies agree?

It has been suggested that there is considerable individual variation in morpheme orders, and that longitudinal and cross-sectional studies do not always agree (Rosansky, 1976). In an attempt to determine just how much variation really exists, I recently reviewed every study available to me where grammatical morphemes were analyzed in obligatory occasions. This included child L1, child L2, delayed L1, and adult agrammatics. It included both grouped and individual studies, and longitudinal and cross-sectional studies. The complete list of reports consulted is given in Table 1.

Following de Villiers (1974) I only included morphemes with at least ten obligatory occasions in a given study. This is an extremely small number, and I originally thought that this would produce large

Table 1. *Studies analyzing grammatical morphemes in obligatory occasions*

I. Child L1 acquisition
   A. Individual cross-sectional: none.
   B. Individual longitudinal: Brown, 1973 (Adam, Eve, Sarah); Curtiss, Fromkin, and Krashen, 1978 (Genie).
   C. Grouped cross-sectional: de Villiers and de Villiers, 1973; Kessler, 1975.
   D. Grouped longitudinal: Brown, 1973.

II. Child L2 acquisition
   A. Individual cross-sectional: Kessler and Idar, 1977 (Than, three cross-sections); Rosansky, 1976 (Jorge, ten cross-sections, Marta, Cheo, Juan).
   B. Individual longitudinal: Rosansky, 1976 (Jorge); Hakuta, 1974 (Uguisu); Kessler and Idar, 1977 (Than).
   C. Grouped cross-sectional: Dulay and Burt, 1973; Dulay and Burt, 1974a.

III. Adult L2 acquisition
   A. Individual cross-sectional: Birnbaum, 1976 (Hector); Strei, 1976 (Gerardo); Holdich, 1976 (Holdich); Rosansky, 1976 (Alberto, Dolores).
   B. Individual longitudinal: none.
   C. Grouped cross-sectional: Bailey, Madden, and Krashen, 1974; Larsen-Freeman, 1975; Krashen, Houck, Giunchi, Bode, Birnbaum, and Strei, 1977; Andersen, 1976; Birnbaum, Butler, and Krashen, 1977 (also in Krashen, Butler, Birnbaum, and Robertson, 1978).

IV. Agrammatics
   A. Individual cross-sectional: de Villiers, 1974 (A3, 50, 14, 5, 24, 6, 43 (two cross-sections)).
   B. Individual longitudinal: none.
   C. Grouped cross-sectional: de Villiers, 1974.

variation; just one additional correct response, for example, could change a subject's score on a morpheme by 10 percentage points. Nevertheless, I found an amazing amount of uniformity across all studies that used Monitor-free instruments, that is, in all studies where language was used for communication. (Rosansky (1976), it should be noted, allowed items to be analyzed that appeared in less than ten obligatory occasions for an individual cross-section. This probably accounts for our different conclusions, which are based on some of the same data.)

Table 2 lists the particular relations discovered and describes the criteria for selection. The counterexamples to these generalizations (Table 3) are rarely "serious". As Table 3 indicates, they often fall within 10 percentage points, are items represented by less than twenty obligatory occasions, or are within one or two ranks where percen-

Table 2. *Ordering relations among grammatical morphemes*

I. Clear cases (true at least 90 per cent of the time. Data from studies where each morpheme occurs in at least ten obligatory occasions. Counterexamples discussed in Table 3.)
1. ING precedes Irr. PAST
2. ING precedes Reg. PAST
3. ING precedes III singular
4. ING precedes POSS
5. ING precedes AUX
6. PLURAL precedes Irr. PAST
7. PLURAL precedes Reg. PAST
8. PLURAL precedes III singular
9. PLURAL precedes POSS
10. COP precedes Irr. PAST
11. COP precedes Reg. PAST
12. COP precedes III singular
13. COP precedes POSS
14. ART precedes POSS
15. ART precedes III singular
16. ART precedes Reg. PAST
17. AUX precedes POSS
18. AUX precedes III singular
(1 through 9 hold for all studies; 10 through 18 do not necessarily hold for child L1 acquisition)

II. Less clear cases (true of most studies where each morpheme occurs in at least ten obligatory occasions. Except where indicated, probability of relation holding significant by sign test.)
1. ING precedes ART
2. ING precedes PLURAL
3. PLURAL precedes AUX
4. PLURAL precedes ART $(p < 15)$
5. COP precedes AUX
6. COP precedes ART
7. ART precedes Irr. PAST
8. AUX precedes Irr. PAST
9. AUX precedes Reg. PAST
10. Irr. PAST precedes III singular
11. Irr. PAST precedes Reg. PAST $(p < 0.21)$
12. Irr. PAST precedes POSS $(p < 0.11)$
(Numbers 1, 3, and 7 hold for child L1 acquisition; the others do not necessarily hold for child L1 acquisition.)

---

tages are not given, or come from Uguisu, Hakuta's subject. (Detailed discussion of Uguisu will wait for another study.)

Many of the generalizations hold for L1 as well as L2. In general, this is true of bound morphemes, and this agreement underlies the

Table 3. *Counterexamples to ordering relations among grammatical morphemes*

Total instances consistent with relations given in Table 3 = 881
Total instances inconsistent with relations given in Table 3 = 98 (10%)

Analysis of counterexamples:
(a) within 10 percentage points	= 49 (50%)
(b) within 20 percentage points	= 9
(c) where percentages not given: one rank difference	= 16
(d) where percentages not given: two ranks difference	= 9
(e) studies producing "true" counterexamples (not (a)–(d) above):	
1. Uguisu (Hakuta, 1974)	= 5
2. Larsen-Freeman (Imitation I)	= 2
3. Jorge 11 (Rosansky, 1976)	= 1
4. Dolores (Rosansky, 1976)	= 2
5. Andersen, 1976[a]	= 1
6. agrammatic individual subjects (de Villiers, 1974)[b]	= 4

a: Number of obligatory occasions not known.
b: Obligatory occasions known to be more than ten but may be less than twenty.

consistently positive but often statistically insignificant correlation one sees between L1 and L2 scores when rank order correlations are used.

Figure 1 gives a proposed "natural order" for second language and for Broca's aphasia, and was constructed from the relations given in Table 2. It is extremely interesting to note that all "Monitor-free"

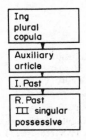

Fig. 1. Proposed "natural order" for second language acquisition and agrammatics

studies using adult subjects (except Imitations I and II; see Larsen-Freeman, 1975, for discussion of Imitation I) show a healthy positive correlation with this order[1] (Table 4).

The data presented here strongly confirm the reality of a "natural order", a reliably occurring order in longitudinal and cross-sectional,

Table 4. *Rank order correlations with the proposed "natural order"*

I. Studies with nine countable grammatical morphemes:

Study[a]	Rank order correlation[b]
Marta	0.823
Uguisu	0.170
Dulay and Burt, 1974b—combined	0.770
Dulay and Burt, 1974b—Spanish	0.753
Dulay and Burt, 1974b—Chinese	0.827
Dolores	0.849
Andersen, 1976	0.883
Larsen-Freeman, BSM time I	0.840
Larsen-Freeman, BSM time II	0.857
Larsen-Freeman, Imitation I	0.416
Larsen-Freeman, Imitation II	0.719
Larsen-Freeman, Listen I	0.719
Larsen-Freeman, Listen II	0.606
Larsen-Freeman, Read I	0.130
Larsen-Freeman, Read II	−0.130
Larsen-Freeman, Write I	0.217
Larsen-Freeman, Write II	0.148

for $n = 9$, significance at 0.05 level requires rho = 0.600 or larger.
significance at 0.01 level requires rho = 0.783 or larger.

II. Studies with eight countable grammatical morphemes:

Study	Rank order correlation
Jorge 7	0.878
Jorge 11	0.615
Jorge 18	0.725
Jorge 20	0.886
Dulay and Burt, 1973—Sacramento	0.939
Dulay and Burt, 1973—East Harlem	0.878
Dulay and Burt, 1973—San Ysidro	0.865
Bailey, Madden, and Krashen, 1974	0.939
Krashen, Houck, et al., 1977	0.779

for $n = 8$, significance at 0.05 level requires rho = 0.643 or larger.
significance at 0.01 level requires rho = 0.833 or larger.   (*continued*)

individual and grouped studies of second language performers. Admittedly, it is not a rigidly invariant order, as shown in Fig. 1. It is also far from random, however.

The task is far from complete in this area. As indicated in Table 1, more data should be gathered for adults longitudinally, and the effect of monitoring on the morpheme order deserves replication.

Table 4 (*cont.*)

III. Studies with seven countable grammatical morphemes:

Study	Rank order correlation
Cheo	0.712
Juan	0.368
Jorge 9	0.769
Jorge 13	0.862
Jorge 15	0.726
Holdich	0.726
Alberto	0.730
Birnbaum *et al.*, Free I	0.726
Birnbaum *et al.*, Edit. I	0.802
Birnbaum *et al.*, Free II	0.557
Birnbaum *et al.*, Edit. II	0.712
de Villiers, 1974—agrammatics combined	0.880
Agrammatics:	
A3	0.955
A50	0.599
A14	0.962
A43 time I	0.749
A43 time II	0.755
A5	0.637
A24	0.768
A6	0.805

for $n = 7$, significance at 0.05 level requires 0.714 or larger.
significance at 0.01 level requires 0.893 or larger.
(one-tail)

a: All individual cross-sections listed, with the exception of Uguisu (Hakuta, 1974) and Holdich (Holdich, 1976), and the agrammatics, are from Rosansky (1976).
b: All correlations have been corrected for ties.

A final objection that has been raised is that merely dealing with morphemes in obligatory occasions may fail to reveal at least some aspects of language acquisition, the overgeneralizations, and the *transitional* forms that acquirers go through. This is, I think, perfectly true, but does not detract at all from the validity of the results of the morpheme studies. The observed morpheme order is the result of the interplay of the underlying process of acquisition, and they only show the product, the surface order of acquisition. They do not directly reveal the pathway the acquirer took in arriving there. Nevertheless, there is no reason to assume the obtained order is invalid; it has been shown to be highly reliable, and occurs, for the adult, in predictable situations; there is, as yet, no counterevidence to the hypothesis that the existence of the natural order in the adult is indeed a manifestation of the creative construction process, or language acquisition.[2]

Notes

[1] Kendall W (coefficient of concordance) was computed for those studies containing the same morphemes in the minimum number of obligatory occasions. For studies with nine morphemes in common (Marta, Uguisu, Dulay and Burt, 1974—combined, Dolores, Andersen, 1976, and Larsen-Freeman's two administrations of the BSM), $W = 0.619$, $p < 0.001$. For studies with the same morphemes in common (Jorge 7, 11, 18, 20, Krashen et al., 1977), $W = 0.64$, $p < 0.01$. For studies with the same seven morphemes in common (Birnbaum, Butler, and Krashen, 1977—Free I, Edit. I, Free II, Edit. II, Cheo, Alberto), $W = 0.618$, $p < 0.01$. de Villiers (1974) computed a Kendall W of 0.60 ($p = 0.001$) for her individual agrammatic subjects.

The relationships proposed in Fig. 1 are also supported in Andersen (1977), who reanalyzed his 1975 data in several interesting ways. Andersen also presents data indicating significant agreement among individual subjects. Additional evidence against excessive individual variation is Bailey et al. (1974), who found "a high level of agreement" among different classes of ESL students for grammatical morpheme difficulty order. Each subgroup contained about ten students.

While all correlations with the "natural order" for Monitor-free studies are positive, a few miss statistical significance at the 0.05 level. This is occasionally due to unusual performance in one morpheme: in Juan, for example, there was very high performance in the III singular morpheme (16/16). In my judgment, this failure to reach significance in every case is not serious, as several studies that "miss" come quite close (e.g. Cheo) and the effect is reliable. See Ferguson (1971), among others, for a discussion of the prevalence of type II errors when such near misses are analyzed as non-rejection of the null hypothesis when n's are small, as here.

[2] Wode, Bahns, Bedey, and Frank (1978) discuss several "shortcomings of the morpheme order approach" which deserve repeating. First, they correctly point out that any approach that focuses exclusively on "the relative chronology of target-like mastery of several items . . . necessarily misses all developments leading toward and preceding the final state of achievement" (p. 181). Wode et al.'s data from child second language acquisition, along with earlier studies in L1 acquisition, illustrate quite clearly that the study of transitional competence, the intermediate structures performers use on their way to "target-like mastery", reveals an enormous amount about language acquisition that focusing on final forms misses. Second, Wode et al. claim that "morpheme order studies" miss avoidance phenomena. A good example is provided by Wode et al.'s subject, who produced no constructions of the sort

$$N + 's + N$$

where the first N is not a name. That is, they would produce utterances like

Johnny's dog

but not

the cat's ear

in English. Wode et al. suggest that the reason for this avoidance is the fact that such constructions are ungrammatical in the L1, German:

Heikos Angel (Heiko's fishing pole)

but
*der Katze Ohr (the cat's ear).

While control data would make Wode *et al.*'s argument even more convincing (e.g. ESL with other first languages or English as a first language), their explanation is quite plausible.

Wode *et al.* also point out that use of cross-sectional techniques, as opposed to longitudinal, fail to make the distinction between true mastery and what Wode *et al.* call "premature forms". For example, in their data, subjects would first produce forms like "feet", "sheep", and "fish" correctly in the plural, without the /s/ ending. Somewhat later, however, the children would incorrectly add the /s/ marker to these forms, with the correct form re-emerging later. The phenomenon of premature forms is well attested in first language acquisition (Ervin, 1964; Cazden, 1972). While Wode *et al.*'s point is reasonable, the empirical evidence suggests that the existence of premature forms does not seriously affect the validity of cross-sectional studies, as the agreement between cross-sectional and longitudinal orders is quite high, when sufficient samples are used.

Finally, Wode *et al.* note that ordering studies might be overly concerned with determining relative order of acquisition of items that are formally quite different. For example, one would not be interested in the relative order of /r/ and negation.

Similarly, Wode *et al.* suggest that bound and free forms might be "acquisitionally quite different" (p. 184). This is precisely what we have found (Krashen *et al.*, 1978); with bound forms showing very clearly consistency across children and adults, L1 and L2, while free forms, which are ordered among themselves with some consistency, appear relatively "later" in L1 acquisition.

Wode *et al.* conclude that both acquisition order and "developmental sequence" (or "transitional competence") studies "focus on different aspects of the total process of L2 acquisition . . . therefore, the conclusion cannot be to claim general superiority of one over the other" (p. 184).

5. The Role of the First Language in Second Language Acquisition

The topic of "first language interference" has had an unusual history in second language acquisition research and practice. For many years, it had been presumed that the only major source of syntactic errors in adult second language performance was the performer's first language (Lado, 1957), and a great deal of materials preparation was done with this assumption in mind (Banathy, Trager, and Waddle, 1966). Subsequent empirical studies of errors made by second language students led to the discovery, however, that many errors are not traceable to the structure of the first language, but are common to second language performers of different linguistic backgrounds (e.g. Richards, 1971; Buteau, 1970). These findings have led several scholars to question the value of contrastive analysis and to argue instead for error analysis. The first language, it is maintained, is but one of several sources of error, and other sources need to be considered.

The issue now, as I see it, is not whether first-language-influenced errors exist in second language performance (they clearly do), or even what percentage of errors can be traced to the first language in the adult, but, rather, where first language influence fits in the theoretical model for second language performance.

In this chapter, I will attempt to show that findings on first language influence on second language performance are quite consistent with findings and hypotheses from other apparently nonrelated areas, and that they contribute to a clear theoretical picture of second language acquisition and performance. First, the relevant findings on first language influence are summarized. Following this, the role of the first language *as a substitute utterance initiator* is discussed.

64

Research Findings

1. First language influence appears to be strongest in complex word order and in word-for-word translations of phrases.

Evidence for this generalization comes from several sources. Duškova (1969), for example, studied written errors in the compositions of Czech "postgraduate students" and concluded that "interference from the mother tongue . . . was plainly obvious in errors of word order and sentence construction" (p. 18), a common example being the placement of the direct object after an adverbial, as in

> I met there some Germans.

Also present in the compositions were many word-for-word translations of Czech expressions into English, such as "another my friend" instead of "another friend of mine".

LoCoco (1975), in a study of American college students learning Spanish and German in the US, a foreign language situation, reported that the "high incidence of interlingual (L1 interference) errors in German was due to word order errors . . ." (p. 101). Typical examples include

	Hoffentlich du bist gesund
	Hopefully you are healthy
correct:	Hoffentlich bist du gesund

and

	Ich bin glücklich sein hier
	I am happy to be here
correct:	Ich bin glücklich hier zu sein.

First-language-based errors in Spanish were less numerous and "pertained primarily to adjective position". The greater word differences between English and German as compared to English and Spanish accounts for the differences in frequencies in interference word order errors. Spanish students were more often correct in using English surface structures in utterance initiation due to the greater surface similarity between English and Spanish. This also accounts for Chan's (1975) finding that English to Spanish interference errors occurred mainly "on grammatical categories absent in either the NL or TL" and not in word order.

LoCoco also found that second level Spanish students showed an increase in interference type errors that LoCoco calls "whole expression terms", or word-for-word translations of an L1 expression, which is similar to what Duškova reported.

2. First language influence is weaker in bound morphology.

Duškova (1969) notes that errors in bound morphology (e.g. omission of plurals on nouns, lack of subject–verb agreement, adjective–noun agreement) are not due to first language influence in her Czech students of EFL: Czech nouns do not distinguish singular and plural and in Czech "the finite verb agrees with its subject in person and number". These errors are, rather, "interference between the other terms of the English subsystem in question" (p. 21). Moreover, these errors "occur even in cases where the English form is quite analogous to the corresponding Czech form" (p. 21). Of 166 morphological errors, only nineteen were judged as due to Czech interference. (Interestingly, of these nineteen, several were free morphemes; see discussion in Chapter 4.)

Also consistent is Kellerman's (forthcoming) suggestion that inflectional morphology ("except in very closely related languages") belongs to the category of structures that performers generally do not transfer in second language performance.

3. First language influence seems to be strongest in "acquisition-poor" environments.

Dulay and Burt (1974b) and Gillis and Weber (1976) have demonstrated that first language influence is rare in child second language acquisition (but see below). On the other hand, studies that report a high amount of first language influence, such as those cited above, are mostly foreign and not second language studies, situations in which natural appropriate intake is scarce and where translation exercises are frequent. In this regard, it is interesting to note that we can find signs of first language influence in immersion bilingual programs where input is often primarily from the teacher and not from peers.

First-language-influenced errors here are also in the domain of word order (Selinker, Swain, and Dumas, 1975; Plann and Ramirez, 1976).

This suggests that it is not simply the case that adults show first language influence while children do not. We would expect to see first language influence in situations where child second language acquirers obtain less intake or where affective conditions prevent or inhibit acquisition (where the affective filter "filters" the input; see Chapter 2).

Conclusions

We now attempt to integrate these findings and fit them into the Monitor Model for performance. First, let us reconsider Newmark's (1966) proposal for a mechanism for first language influence. According to Newmark, first language influence is not proactive inhibition, but is simply the result of the performer being "called on to perform before he has learned the new behavior". The result is "padding", using old knowledge, supplying what is known to make up for what is not known. Newmark suggests that the "cure for interference is simply the cure for ignorance: learning" (in terms of Monitor Theory, this would read "acquisition").

What can be concluded from the above is that the L1 may "substitute" for the acquired L2 as an utterance initiator when the performer has to produce in the target language but has not acquired enough of the L2 to do this. It may in fact be the case that the domain in L2 performance is the same as those rules that are most prone to L1 influence, while aspects of the target language that may be learned (late acquired, easy to conceptualize; e.g. bound morphology) are relatively free of L1 influence.

First language influence may therefore be an indication of low acquisition. If so, it can be eliminated or at least reduced by natural intake and language use. This is what apparently occurred in Taylor's ESL subjects, who showed less first language influence with more proficiency (Taylor, 1975).

Perhaps the "silent period" observed in natural child second language acquisition (Hakuta, 1974; Huang and Hatch, 1978) corresponds to the period in which the first language is heavily used in "unnatural" adult second language performance. The children may be building up acquired competence via input, and several recent studies (Gary, 1974; Postovsky, 1977) imply that less insistence on early oral performance may be profitable for children and adults studying second languages in formal settings.

The L1 plus Monitor Mode

First language influence can thus be considered as unnatural. One could theoretically produce sentences in a second language without any acquisition: the first language surface structure can be used with second language content lexicon inserted. The Monitor may then be used to add some morphology and do its best to repair word order where it differs from the L1. One can only go so far with this mode, as one is limited by the competence of the conscious grammar and one must appeal to it with every utterance. The adult can, however, produce sentences right away in the target language using this mode, and this may help to account for reports of more rapid progress in early stages for adults than for children in second language performance (Snow and Hoefnagel-Hohle, 1978). It is a temporary advantage, however. Acquisition may be slow, but it is, in the long run, much more useful when language is used for the purpose of communication.[1]

Note

[1] Several recent papers point out that the hypothesis presented here, that we "fall back" on the first language when we have not acquired aspects of the second language, as stated here, is inadequate to account for all of the data. As Wode (1978) has pointed out, first-language-influenced errors may only occur at certain stages in development. Wode's example is quite clear, and is reviewed here.

In English, the negative particle appears after the auxiliary, as in

(1) I can not go,

but before main verbs, with do-support, as in

(2) I don't know.

In German, however, the negative particle appears after both auxiliaries and main verbs, as in

(3) Ich kann nicht gehen,
    I   can   not   go,

and   (4) Ich weiss nicht,
        I   know   not.

Wode's children, German-speakers acquiring English as a second language in the United States, produced some sentences showing apparent first language influence, such as

(5) John go not to the school.

What is interesting, Wode points out, is that they did not produce such sentences early on. Their first attempts at negation were similar to what one sees in first language acquisition, such as

(6) no, you,
(7) no play baseball.

They only produced sentences such as (5) when they had begun to acquire the aux. + neg. rule, i.e. when they had begun to produce sentences such as

(8) lunch is no ready.

Only then did they "fall back" on the more general German rule. Wode (1978, 1979) suggests that there is, therefore, a structural prerequisite for first language influence: the performer's interlinguistic structural description, his idea of the target language rule, must be similar to the structural description of the rule in his first language. Wode's children's English negation rule was not at all similar to the German rule in early stages, but it became similar when they progressed to the aux.–neg. stage. Hence, first language influence appeared later, but not earlier.

Also consistent with his argument is the fact that sentences such as (5) are only found in child second language acquisition of English when the first language has post-verbal negation, as in Ravem (1968), in which the first language was Norwegian. Such sentences were not observed in other ESL studies utilizing different first languages (Milon, 1974, L1 = Japanese) and in studies of negation in English as a first language.

Kellerman (1978) suggests another condition for "transfer" to occur. The acquirer must *perceive* a similarity between items in the first and second language. Items that appear to be language specific (e.g. idioms) will be less prone to transfer.

These conditions are not contrary to the generalization presented here. It can still be maintained that we "fall back" on the first language when we have not acquired aspects of the second language. They show, however, that ignorance is not a sufficient condition for the occurrence of first language influence.

6. The Neurological Correlates of Language Acquisition: Current Research

Research and speculation on the neurological correlates of language acquisition have been growing at a rapid and accelerating rate, and it is increasingly difficult for the nonspecialist to adequately cover and evaluate current discoveries. This paper will attempt to review some of the current research in this area, that dealing with what is perhaps the most obvious neurological phenomenon relating to language, cerebral dominance, or lateralization, and attempt to update the reader on recent progress and suggest some interpretations of this research.

Cerebral Dominance

It is by now a well-established finding that for most people (practically all right-handers and most left-handers), the two sides of the cortex perform different functions. As Table 1 indicates, the left hemisphere

Table 1. *Functions of the two hemispheres*

Left hemisphere	Right hemisphere
Language	Spatial relations
Time-related functions	"Gestalt" perception
	Part-to-whole judgments
"Propositional" thought	Music
	"Appositional" thought

is responsible for most linguistic performance in adults. Recent studies strongly suggest that the left brain is also involved in certain non-linguistic functions, specifically those related to the perception of *time*: for example, the left hemisphere is superior to the right in judging temporal order, or deciding which of two stimuli was presented first (see, for example, Carmon and Nachshon, 1971; Papcun, Krashen, Terbeek, Remington, and Harshman, 1974). The "other side of the

70

brain", the right hemisphere, appears to be responsible for spatial relations, so-called "gestalt" perception (exemplified by the ability to rapidly estimate the number of dots on a card after an extremely brief exposure, without actually counting each dot), and "part-to-whole" judgments (for example, matching arcs to circles). At least some aspects of musical perception may also be done by the right hemisphere (Milner, 1962).

The eminent neurosurgeon, Joseph Bogen, in a fascinating series of papers (Bogen, 1969a, 1969b; Bogen and Bogen, 1969), has speculated that the two sides of the brain utilize two different cognitive modes, one "propositional" (analytic, digital) and one "appositional" (analogic, synthetic). Only the intactness of the corpus callosum, the fibres connecting the two hemispheres, allows us the illusion that we have just one mind.

A variety of techniques have been used by researchers to ascertain "where things are" in the brain. At one time, researchers had to depend on "natural experiments", the unfortunate consequences of unilateral brain damage caused by tumor, strokes and man-made accidents (e.g. gunshot wounds). Correlations were made between the locus of a lesion and the type of impairment the patient suffered: for example, we know that in adults, aphasia is nearly always the result of injury to the left hemisphere (Russell and Espir, 1961, report that 97 per cent of their 205 aphasics had left hemisphere damage).

While researchers continue to rely on data from brain damage to a large extent, more recently laterality in normal subjects has been investigated using several harmless techniques. In *dichotic listening*, subjects are presented with competing, simultaneous auditory stimuli (e.g. the right ear hears "ba" while the left ear hears "ga"). A right-ear advantage in response accuracy is thought to reflect left hemisphere processing for the stimulus presented. In adults, dichotic presentation of verbal stimuli typically results in a right-ear advantage (Kimura, 1961), while certain non-verbal stimuli (environmental sounds, musical chords; see Curry, 1967; Gordon, 1970) yield a left-ear advantage. The right-ear advantage for verbal stimuli typically seen in normal subjects is generally quite small, but it is reliable, and, when groups of subjects are used, it is usually statistically significant.

Other techniques include the use of EEG and AER (average evoked response). When verbal stimuli are used, subjects typically show a higher evoked response in the left hemisphere, indicating greater processing activity (Wood, Goff, and Day, 1971). In EEG studies, verbal stimulation results in depressed alpha wave activity in the left hemisphere (the presence of alpha waves indicates a resting or meditative state) (Morgan, McDonald, and MacDonald, 1971).

The Development of Cerebral Dominance and Language Acquisition

Much of the controversy on the issue of the neurology of language acquisition is concerned with the development of cerebral dominance in childhood and its relation to language acquisition, both in first and second languages. The history of this issue begins with Lenneberg (1967), who hypothesized that the development of cerebral dominance was complete by around puberty ("firmly established"). According to Lenneberg, the infant brain is not firmly lateralized; in case of damage to the left hemisphere, or in case of removal of the left hemisphere ("hemispherectomy"), the right hemisphere is able to assume the language function. Lenneberg presented evidence that suggested that this ability of the language function to "transfer" hemispheres lasts until puberty, a conclusion that appeared to be consistent with reports of better recovery from acquired aphasia in children under age 10 or so. After puberty, the right hemisphere did not appear to be able to assume the language function in case of injury to or removal of the left hemisphere and Lenneberg hypothesized that this was due to the fact that lateralization of language to the left hemisphere was now complete. The presence of some of the language function in the right hemisphere in children also might be responsible for their superior recovery from aphasia.

Lenneberg (see also Scovel, 1969) also hypothesized that the end of the development of cerebral dominance coincided with the close of a "critical period" for language acquisition, noting that "foreign accents cannot be overcome easily after puberty" (p. 176) and that "automatic acquisition (of second languages) from mere exposure . . . seems to disappear after this age" (p. 176). Lenneberg therefore proposed a biological explanation for child–adult differences in language acquisition attainment, a very serious claim for those of us interested in second language acquisition in adults and one which could imply lowered expectancies on the part of both teachers and students.

Since 1967, however, there have been some encouraging research reports. While there seems to be no question that puberty is an important turning point in language acquisition (see, for example, Seliger, Krashen, and Ladefoged, 1975), it is not at all clear that the development of cerebral dominance is directly related. Second, alternative explanations are available to explain child–adult differences, explanations that are far more encouraging than the biological one. We will first briefly review the "state of research" over the last decade on the question of the development of cerebral dominance, and then review one of these alternative explanations.

Simply, it is no longer clear that the development of cerebral dominance is complete at puberty. There are now arguments supporting the position that lateralization is "firmly established" much earlier, at least by age 5, and that the preconditions for lateralization may be present even at birth. Below, we briefly summarize the experimental and clinical literature that has appeared on this topic in the last few years. As we shall see, most of the reports support "early" lateralization. There are, however, some apparent inconsistencies that we discuss below.

1. *Dichotic listening.* Witelson (1977) has reviewed all known studies using dichotic listening with children and concludes that ". . . of 36 experiments, 30, or about 83 per cent, reported right-ear superiority for their youngest subgroups, and all found right-ear superiority in at least older subgroups" (p. 230) (where "younger" indicates from about age 3 to about 7). Studies evaluating developmental trends usually report no increase in degree of lateralization over time (age), supporting the hypothesis that language lateralization is firmly established far earlier than puberty. A few studies, however, do in fact report an increasing right-ear advantage up to about puberty, consistent with Lenneberg's position. What is interesting about these studies (e.g. Satz, Bakker, Teunissen, Goebel, and Van der Vlugt, 1975) is that the stimuli used for dichotic presentation were slightly different from the stimuli used in studies that report no change in degree of lateralization with increasing age. In the "puberty" studies, the children were presented with two or three sets of digits at one time

(e.g. the pair "2" (right ear) and "9" (left ear) would be presented, followed one half-second later by "6" (right ear) and "4" (left ear), followed by "1" (right ear) and "3" (left ear). The subject is asked to recall as many digits as possible out of the six presented.) In most other studies, one single pair of syllables (e.g. "ba" and "ga") or words were used, a lower short-term memory load. This raises the possibility that there might be two different developmental courses for two different kinds of language processing, one complete lateralized to the left hemisphere by puberty and the other much earlier in life.

2. *Motor skills.* Early completion of the development of cerebral dominance is also indicated by studies examining the development of unimanual motor skills. Caplan and Kinsbourne (1976), in a paper appropriately titled "Baby drops the rattle", provide an interesting example. The experimenters gave rattles to twenty-one infants (average age 21 months, 21 days) and found that the babies tended to hold the rattles longer when they were placed in their right hands (average duration of grasp = 62 seconds for the right hand and 41 seconds for the left hand), suggesting early lateral specialization of the central nervous system. Witelson (1977) has reviewed many studies of this sort using children age 7 and younger and concludes that "right-hand or right-sided superiority was observed in the large majority of the 34 studies" (p. 236). This supports the hypothesis that there is an early propensity for unimanual performance of motor tasks, which is consistent with the hypothesis that cerebral dominance is established early in life.

3. *Brain damage.* Studies examining the effects of unilateral brain damage on language in children also imply that lateralization is complete earlier than puberty. In later childhood (age 5 and older), just as in adults, aphasia is primarily the result of *left* hemisphere lesions. It appears to be the case, however, that before age 5 aphasia may result from right hemisphere lesions somewhat more frequently (about 30 per cent of the time, as compared with 3 per cent in adults and older children). Still, even for very young children, aphasia is associated more often with left lesions than with right lesions (for reviews, see Witelson, 1977; Krashen, 1973a; Hécean, 1976).

4. *Hemispherectomy.* The removal of an entire hemisphere, hemispherectomy, is perhaps the ultimate test of laterality. If the left

hemisphere is removed, and the patient is still able to speak, we can assume that the right hemisphere had at least some part in the language function before the surgery. The literature indicates that early removal of the left hemisphere for lesions incurred before age 5 does *not* generally result in aphasia. This result, like the data from unilateral lesions ((3) above) implies at least some right hemisphere participation in the language function in early years (Krashen, 1973a; Witelson, 1977).

The hemispherectomy data are clear only up to age 5 (Krashen, 1973a), as this surgical procedure is rarely used with older children. *5. EEG and AER.* Research using EEG and AER techniques suggest that signs of hemispheric specialization are present even at birth. When infants as young as 2 weeks old are presented with verbal stimuli (e.g. the mother's voice), the auditory evoked response is greater over the left hemisphere; when musical stimuli are presented (e.g. a music box), the AER is greater over the right hemisphere (Molfese, 1976). EEG results are similar: we see left–right differences in infants as young as 5 months old (Gardiner and Walter, 1976).

6. Some researchers have looked for anatomical differences between the two hemispheres: slight differences do in fact exist in the adult brain (Geschwind and Levitsky, 1968) and it has been confirmed that similar left–right morphological differences exist in the infant and even in the pre-natal brain (Witelson and Pallie, 1973; Wada, Clarke, and Hamm, 1975), suggesting at least the potential or predisposition for hemispheric specialization.

What can we conclude about the development of cerebral dominance from this array of reports? We have seen some evidence for "lateralization by zero" (consistent with EEG, AER, and anatomical studies, as well as some dichotic listening studies and experiments using unimanual motor skills), some for "lateralization by 5" (clinical data on brain damage and hemispherectomy) and some for lateralization by puberty (dichotic studies using more difficult stimuli). A possible solution is to posit the following developmental course:

1. Most of us are born with a predisposition for left hemisphere language, and there is thus some specialization right from the start, enough to be detected by EEG and AER, and to influence the development of unimanual motor skills.

2. This degree of lateralization increases until about age 5, by which time most aspects of language processing are lateralized to the left hemisphere at the adult level. This accounts for the brain damage and hemispherectomy data, which show some right hemisphere contribution to the language function before age 5.
3. Certain aspects of language are not entirely lateralized to the left hemisphere until later, perhaps by puberty. These aspects of linguistic competence may be those that are necessary for the perception of longer and more complex stimuli. This accounts for the exceptional dichotic listening studies.[1]

Whether or not this particular schema is the correct one, one clear conclusion that can be drawn from this literature survey is that there is little doubt that children show left hemisphere dominance for much of the language function well before puberty. There is also no necessary relationship between cerebral dominance and second language acquisition ability. As mentioned above, alternative explanations have been proposed for child–adult differences in second language attainment, explanations that are probably unrelated to cerebral dominance. As an example we briefly sketch one possibility.

In Chapter 2 it was hypothesized that certain cognitive and affective changes taking place around puberty, possibly connected to the onset of the stage of formal operations (Inhelder and Piaget, 1958), an event which generally occurs at around age 12, may have the effect of boosting language *learning* potential, while limiting or weakening the language *acquisition* potential. This change may be responsible for observed child–adult differences in language acquisition.

At formal operations, the adolescent becomes an abstract thinker, and is able to "reflect on the rules he possesses and on his thoughts" (*Developmental Psychology Today*, 1971, p. 336). He can, for the first time, "take his mental constructions as objects and reason about them", and can "deal with problems in which many factors operate at the same time" (Elkind, 1970, p. 66).

The meta-awareness and ability to theorize brought about by formal operations allows the learner (or compels him) to create an abstract theory (or grammar) of the language he is approaching. Formal operations may thus allow the "conscious grammar", or

Monitor, to exist, and the degree to which one has become a formal thinker may relate to the success one has in formal language learning.

On the other hand, formal operations may be at least partly responsible for a fossilization of progress in subconscious language acquisition. One effect of formal operations on acquisition may be a result of what can be termed the indirect effects of formal operations, namely the affective changes that occur in adolescence that are catalyzed by formal operations. These changes result in the self-consciousness and feelings of vulnerability often observed in this age group. Elkind (1970) has argued that formal operations allows one to conceptualize the thoughts of others—this leads the adolescent to the false conclusions that others are thinking about him and are focusing on just what he considers to be his inadequacies. Such feelings may generate at least in part attitudes unfavorable for the successful acquisition of a second language, which may act to discourage the acquirer from interacting with primary linguistic data, and/or may act to strengthen an "affective filter" (Dulay and Burt, 1977) that prevents the acquirer from utilizing all the input he hears for further language acquisition. (For more detailed discussion, see Chapter 2.)

The available data strongly suggest, however, that subconscious language acquisition is nevertheless the central means by which adults internalize second languages, a position supported not only by research but also by the practice of successful language teachers who emphasize communicative activities in the classroom (see, for example, Terrell, 1977).

To summarize to this point: Lenneberg's claim that lateralization was complete by puberty and is the neurological basis for the critical period for language acquisition and thus responsible for child–adult differences in second language acquisition is not entirely ruled out. There is, however, considerable evidence today that implies that much of the development of cerebral dominance may be complete much earlier and may have little or nothing to do with the critical period. Moreover, there are other possible "explanations" for the critical period. The one sketched above maintains that the ability to "acquire" language naturally does not disappear at puberty, a position that is consistent with current teaching practice.

The Role of the Right Hemisphere in Second Language Acquisition

We turn now to a slightly different but related topic, one that has also stimulated a great deal of interest recently: the role of the right hemisphere in second language acquisition. The position we outlined for first language acquisition is consistent with the idea that the right hemisphere may play some role in early stages, and interestingly enough, it has been suggested that the right brain is somehow involved in normal second language acquisition in much the same way. Again, we briefly list some recent research results in this area, and attempt to supply an explanation.

1. *Brain damage.* In a recent survey of aphasia in "polyglot" subjects, Galloway (forthcoming) found a slightly higher incidence of aphasia due to right-sided lesions than in a presumably monolingual population (Table 2), consistent with the idea that the right hemisphere might be playing some role in second language acquisition or performance.

Table 2. *Frequency of aphasia in polyglots and monolinguals*

	Right-handers		Left-handers	
	polyglots	monolinguals*	polyglots	monolinguals*
Right lesions	4 (14%)	2%	5 (71%)	32%
Left lesions	25 (86%)	98%	2 (29%)	68%

* Estimated from aphasia literature (Galloway, forthcoming).

2. *Dichotic listening and tachistoscopic exposure.* Some dichotic listening studies and some tachistoscopic exposure studies (a visual analogue of dichotic listening: response superiority for items flashed to the right visual field is interpreted as reflecting left hemisphere processing) show little or no difference between first and second languages, typically showing left hemisphere processing for both (Hamers and Lambert, 1977; Barton, Goodglass, and Shai, 1965; Kershner and Jeng, 1972; Carroll, 1978). Other studies, however, do show the second language to be less left hemisphere lateralized or show right hemisphere processing. Obler, Albert, and Gordon (1975), in a study of Hebrew–English bilinguals, found a right-ear advantage for both Hebrew and English words, but observed a greater right-ear

advantage in the first language. English-dominant Americans acquiring Hebrew in Israel displayed a greater right-ear advantage for English words than for Hebrew, and Hebrew-dominant Israelis who learned some English in school showed a greater right-ear advantage for Hebrew. Gaziel, Obler, Benton, and Albert (1977), in a tachistoscopic study of Israeli students studying English, found results quite consistent with those of Obler *et al.* (1975). As can be seen on Table 3,

Table 3. *Number of subjects showing visual field effect*

	Seventh grade: Hebrew stimuli				English stimuli	
LVFE	0	RVFE	LVFE	0	RVFE
2	1	21	20	1	3
	Ninth grade: Hebrew stimuli				English stimuli	
LVFE	0	RVFE	LVFE	0	RVFE
0	0	24	16	2	6
	Eleventh grade: Hebrew stimuli				English stimuli	
LVFE	0	RVFE	LVFE	0	RVFE
2	1	21	6	5	13

LVFE = left visual field effect (suggests right hemisphere processing).
RVFE = right visual field effect (suggests left hemisphere processing).
0 = no difference in visual field accuracy.

From Gaziel, Obler, Benton, and Albert (1977).

processing of Hebrew words was done by the left hemisphere by most subjects in all 3 years of school. With English, the second language, this was not the case: in grade 7, most subjects showed a left visual field advantage. The number of subjects behaving this way was less in grade 9, and less still in grade 11.

Obler (1980) suggests that these data are most consistent with a *stage hypothesis*. The right hemisphere participates in second language acquisition in early stages. Obler's hypothesis is not at all inconsistent with the findings we have listed above. If the right hemisphere is involved only in initial stages of second language acquisition, we might expect *some* cases of aphasia involving second languages to involve the right hemisphere, which is precisely what Galloway found. Also, it is quite possible that the subjects used in the experiments listed in (2) above that did not show L1–L2 differences utilized subjects of advanced second language competence (probably true of all but Carroll, 1978; see discussion below). Finally, Obler's hypothesis allows a neat parallel between first and second language acquisition, both involving right hemisphere participation in early stages.

There are, however, the inevitable problems and potential counter-examples. In a recent TESOL presentation, Carroll (1978) reported a clear right-ear advantage using dichotic listening for Spanish as a foreign language, the second language in fact appearing to produce a greater right-ear advantage than English, the first language. A possible explanation is that foreign language *learning* may involve the conscious grammar, which may be located in the left hemisphere (but not necessarily in the language areas). Indeed, conscious grammar use may be heavier in the second language than the first language, accounting for the greater right-ear advantage in English. Thus, we might refine the stage hypothesis: it could be proposed that the right hemisphere plays a role in early language *acquisition*, not language *learning*. But this does not solve everything. First, dichotic listening uses words, not sentences: is the conscious grammar called up when only words are perceived in isolation? Also, Carroll reported that those with more "natural" exposure to Spanish before age 6 showed less of a right-ear advantage, which would appear to be consistent with the stage hypothesis, but another older group of "informal" acquirers showed a strong right-ear advantage for the second language. Thus, *age* might be a factor: Carroll (personal communication) reminds us that the Gaziel *et al.* subjects were also fairly young (age 12 in the grade 7 group).

Another potential counter-example is Rogers, TenHouten, Kaplan, and Gardiner (1977). Using EEG with bilingual Hopi children in the United States, they found greater left hemisphere lateralization for English, the *second* language. They interpret their data as being consistent with the hypothesis that the language itself may be responsible for their results, with Hopi directing the performers' attention more to the perceptual field (encouraging more right hemisphere use) while English "orients its users to separation or abstraction from the perceptual field" (p. 2). In this case, it is quite possible that the subjects were past the right hemisphere stage in their acquisition of English, and other factors, such as the one suggested by Rogers *et al.*, influenced the results.

Finally, if the stage hypothesis is supported by subsequent studies, we must determine what the right hemisphere contributes to language acquisition. According to recent research (Zaidel, 1973; Curtiss, 1977) even the mature right hemisphere has a surprisingly rich comprehension lexicon and an understanding of basic semantic relationships. Its linguistic inferiority may be primarily in syntax. Does the right hemisphere bring these lexical and semantic abilities into play during early stages of language acquisition, with the left hemisphere fully taking over only when more advanced syntax is acquired, and/or are other "appositional" abilities used?

Conclusions

The current scene in neurolinguistics is somewhat unsettled, but recent years have seen a number of exciting discoveries and rapid progress. Some crucial issues have not been decided, but there are some conclusions we can conservatively draw:

1. While child–adult differences in second language acquisition potential do exist, the evidence for a biological barrier to successful adult acquisition is lacking. On the contrary, there is abundant reason to maintain that adults are still able to "acquire" language naturally to a great extent.
2. There is some evidence for right hemisphere participation in early stages of first and second language acquisition, suggesting a further L1–L2 parallel (L. Obler, personal communication).

These conclusions lead to no methodological breakthroughs, to no "neurolinguistic method". They are, however, quite consistent with current approaches to second language instruction, approaches developed by concerned teachers independent of theory, that emphasize meaningful and communicative activities that take advantage of the adults' ability to acquire language.[2]

Notes

[1] This schema leaves two unresolved problems. First, Molfese (1976) reports no change in degree of AER asymmetry with age for his infant subjects. This may not conflict with the hypothesis that lateralization develops with age; measured laterality in the infant brain may relate quite differently to "true" underlying laterality (see Krashen, 1975c, for detailed discussion). Another possible problem is Lenneberg's observation that recovery from aphasia is better for those injured before puberty, a finding that seems to imply right hemisphere participation in the language function until that age. Here there are two possibilities: first, recovery need not involve the right hemisphere but may be due to undamaged tissue on the left side assuming the language function (see, for example, Roberts, 1958). Second, if it is indeed the right hemisphere that is responsible for this superiority in recovery, perhaps those late-lateralized aspects of language posited in the text play some role.

[2] A very recent study conducted by my associates Linda Galloway and Robin Scarcella, unpublished at the time of this writing, suggests that early second language acquisition may be just as left hemisphere lateralized as first language. Galloway and Scarcella administered dichotic stimuli (words in English and Spanish) to "informal" beginning adult acquirers of English as a second language. These performers were "picking up" English without the benefit of formal instruction and, presumably, without using conscious learning. Galloway and Scarcella found no significant difference in ear advantage for the first language (Spanish) and the second language (English), with both English and Spanish stimuli yielding a right-ear advantage.

7. On Routines and Patterns in Language Acquisition and Performance

In this chapter we will consider the role of prefabricated routines and patterns in first and second language acquisition and performance. The relationship of these "fixed and semi-fixed" expressions to the development of syntactic structure and their status in performance are issues that are both theoretically interesting and of practical importance in second language teaching.

In defining terms, we distinguish between routines and patterns. *Prefabricated routines* are simply memorized whole utterances or phrases, such as "How are you?" or "Where is your hotel?". A performer may use these without any knowledge at all of their internal structure. Entire lines from memorized dialogues qualify as prefabricated routines, as do expressions learned from foreign language books. Hakuta (1974) has noted that *prefabricated patterns* are distinct from routines. These are partly "creative" and partly memorized wholes; they consist of sentence frames with an open "slot" for a word or a phrase, such as "That's a _____" (pen, knife, banana), or Lyon's (1969) example, "Down with _____". Lyons called such constructions "phrase and sentence schemata", and defined them as "utterances that are grammatically unstructured or only partially structured, but which can yet be combined in sentences according to productive rules" (pp. 177–178). Audio-lingual pattern practice is based on the use of prefabricated patterns.

The issue we will be dealing with here is the relationship of routines and patterns to language acquisition, namely, whether routines and patterns play a direct role in the creative construction process. We can distinguish three different positions with regard to this question:

1. Prefabricated routines may evolve into prefabricated patterns. According to this position, purely propositional language does

not exist and performers rely solely on patterns and routines to communicate.

2. Prefabricated routines may evolve into patterns, but at the same time, independently, the creative construction process develops. This implies that in some situations propositional language may "catch up" with automatic speech—that is, the language acquisition process may "reanalyze" patterns and routines as creative constructions.

3. Prefabricated routines may evolve into prefabricated patterns (as in position 1) and these patterns may evolve directly into creative language. In other words routines and patterns may be ingredients of the creative process.

The following sections will briefly review the literature on routines and patterns in neurolinguistics, child first language acquisition, child second language acquisition, and adult second language. We interpret this literature as fully consistent with only position 2.

Neurolinguistic Status of Automatic Speech

Van Lancker (1972, p. 25) defines automatic speech as "conventional greetings, overused and overlearned expressions (such as 'be careful' and 'first things first'), pause fillers such as 'you know' and 'well', certain idioms, swearing, and other emotional language, perhaps stereotyped questions and answers, commands, . . .". Automatic speech (AS) thus appears to share some of the characteristics of routines and patterns.

The most striking neurolinguistic fact about automatic speech is that AS, as contrasted with propositional language, which is lateralized to the left hemisphere (see Krashen, 1976b, for a review), may be represented in both sides of the brain. That is, automatic speech is localized in both the right and left cerebral hemispheres.

The primary evidence for this is the fact that routines and patterns are often preserved in case of nonfluent (syntactic) aphasia and after left hemispherectomy. Patients who have suffered left brain damage, who have lost the ability to speak, can often use automatic speech, as can those who have undergone removal of the left hemisphere during adulthood. A. Smith (1966) describes a case of a man who underwent left hemispherectomy at age 48. The surgery left him nearly totally speechless:

"E. C.'s attempts to reply to questions immediately after operation were totally unsuccessful. He would open his mouth and utter isolated words, and after apparently struggling to organize words for meaningful speech, recognized his inability and would utter expletives or short emotional phrases (e.g. 'Goddamit'). Expletives and curses were well articulated and clearly understandable. However, he could not repeat single words on command or communicate in 'propositional speech until 10 weeks post-operative." Expressive speech showed some development in E. C., but Smith reported that his creative language was still "severely impaired" 8 months after the operation.

A patient studied by Whitaker (1971) suffering from nonfluent aphasia exhibited an interesting sort of automatic speech behavior: he responded to nearly every question or attempt at conversation with the utterance "What'cha gonno do right now? yea yea". Whitaker points out to the student of neurolinguistics that one cannot use such utterances as data in determining a patient's true linguistic competence ". . . on the basis of (this one) utterance, it would be rather farfetched to assume that L. S. (the patient) had retained the WH-question transformation and correct pronominal reference. . . ." (pp. 145–146).

Thought to be related to automatic speech are "ictal speech mechanisms", words or utterances spoken by psychomotor epileptics during, before, or immediately after seizures. Ictal speech mechanisms consist of stereotyped expressions ("I beg your pardon") and emotional utterances which are spoken out of context. As in the case with AS associated with the right side of the brain as well as the left, Serafatinides and Falconer (1963), in agreement with other studies, found that "of 15 patients with truly ictal speech automatisms 4 were operated on the left side and 11 on the right or recessive side" (p. 345).

The neurolinguistic evidence, then, points to the fact that automatic speech is neurologically different from creative language in that it is localized on both sides of the brain, as opposed to just the left hemisphere, and can be preserved in cases of aphasia. If AS is related to routines and patterns, then routines and patterns may have a fundamentally different mental representation than other kinds of language.

Routines and Patterns in First Language Acquisition

R. Brown (1973), in his study of first language acquisition, noted that some of his subjects' sentences were memorized wholes and patterns. He hypothesized that prefabricated routines in children were the result of very high input frequency of a structure that was, at that time, beyond the child's linguistic maturational level. We cannot improve on Brown and Hanlon's (1970, pp. 50–51) description of this phenomenon (see also Cazden, 1972, p. 110).

> The parents of Adam, Eve, and Sarah did produce certain WH-questions at a very high rate in a period when children did not understand the structure of WH-questions. What happened then? The children learned to produce the two most frequently repeated WH-questions, *What's that?* and *What doing?* on roughly appropriate occasions. Their performance had the kind of rigidity that we have learned to recognize as a sign of incomprehension of structure: they did not produce, as their parents of course did, such structurally close variants as *What are these?* and *Who's that?* and *What is he doing?* When, much later, the children began to produce all manner of WH-questions in the pre-posed form (such as *What he wants*) it was interesting to note that *What's that?* and *What are you doing?* were not at first reconstructed in terms of the new analysis. If the children had generated the sentences in terms of their new rules they ought to have said *What that is?* and *What you are doing?* but instead, they, at first, persisted with the old forms. . . . We suggest that any form that is produced with very high frequency by parents will be somehow represented in the child's performance even if its structure is far beyond him. He will find a way to render a version of it and will also form a notion of the circumstances in which it is used. The construction will become lodged in his speech as an unassimilated fragment. Extensive use of such a fragment probably protects it, for a time, from a reanalysis when the structure relevant to it is finally learned.

Thus, routines appear to be immune to rules at first. This clearly implies that routines are part of a system that is separate from the process generating rule-governed, propositional language. It is also evidence that automatic speech does not "turn into" creative constructions. Rather, the creative construction process evolves independently. This is exactly position 2 as stated above.

Another indication that automatic speech forms are generated by a different process than creative construction is the fact that Brown's subject Adam produced many patterns (such as "It's a _____", and

"That's a _____") which were characterized by very high initial performance. Related propositional forms, Brown notes, show a learning curve with a gradual increase in accuracy over time. Patterns and routines, on the other hand, do not. Brown is thus solidly behind position 2 for children language acquisition. Patterns and routines may develop due to high frequency in input in advance of linguistic maturity, but such automatic speech is independent of the creative construction process; it may fall away in some situations and be reanalyzed by the language acquisition process.

On the other hand, R. Clark (1974), in a paper appropriately titled "Performing without Competence", argues that for some children routines do evolve into patterns which in turn become creative language. In her words, "our research findings suggest that (child's speech) becomes creative through the gradual analysis of the internal structure of sequences which begin as prepackaged routines" (p. 9). Clark's conclusions are based on her analysis of her son Adam (not to be confused with Brown's subject of the same name) who was about 3 years old at the time of the study. Adam, according to Clark, would often use his own or another's previous utterance as constituents for his own utterances. For example,

Adam	*R. C.*
Mummy you go.	Where?
Mummy you go swings.	
	Do you want to get off?
No I want to get on.	(This was an error: Adam meant to say "stay on".)

In addition to this use of patterns, Adam tended to use routines as well, trying to use a phrase in situations close to where he heard it. For example, he would say, "I carry you" when he wanted to be carried, having heard his father say this sentence on numerous occasions.

This use of routines and patterns may not be atypical. Clark, however, suggests that for Adam routines evolve into patterns, consistent with positions 1 and 3 above. For example, when a hot meal was brought to the table

(1) Wait for it to cool

was said, which became a routine for Adam. After several weeks of hearing this, Adam was heard to say

(2) Wait for it to dry

when hanging up a washcloth. Also, many of Adam's long sentences were the result of juxtaposing existing routines. For example,

(3) I want *you to get a biscuit for me*

consists of the pattern "I want _____" plus the underlined portion, which existed as an independent routine for Adam.

Clark claims that routines and patterns were *primary* in Adam's development of language: "In Adam's speech at this time a number of routine sequences seemed to coexist with a few simple productive rules. Many, though not necessarily all, the productive rules originated as invariable routines, which were in use for some time with the original lexical items before new lexical items were inserted" (p. 4). Thus Clark, while not denying the existence of a separate creative construction process, supports position 3 as the central means for language development for Adam. This seems to be in conflict with Brown's conclusion.

The work of A. Peters (1977) helps to resolve this apparent conflict. Peters distinguishes "analytic" and "gestalt" styles of first language development. The analytic style, which is used for referential, labelling functions, is the "one word at a time" development described in most studies of child language acquisition, such as those by Brown and his co-workers. The "gestalt" style, on the other hand, is the attempt to use whole utterances in a socially appropriate situation; it is thus used in more "conversationally defined" contexts. Peters suggests that there is individual variation among children as to which style will predominate. One of the factors that may determine which style a child will prefer is input type: the "analytic" child may have received clear caretaker speech, while the "gestalt" child may have received more rapid, conversational input.

A given child may use one style for one situation and the other for other situations: Peters' subject Minh appeared to speak analytically when naming, and used the gestalt style for social functions. Other investigators (Dore, 1974; Nelson, 1975) have also noted this kind of variation. Nelson, for example, distinguishes a "referential style" used by children who are more oriented to things, objects, and actions on objects from an "expressive" style, used by children who are personal-social oriented. Perhaps the latter is related to Peters' gestalt style and the former to the analytic style.

Peters' analysis is strengthened by Dore's (1974) analysis of two child L1 acquirers, M (female) and J (male). While M produced words during the period her speech was studied, J produced more primitive speech acts, that is, he tended to make more use of language for communication, often using intonation alone. J's language use also tended to involve other people more than M's did; he used language more instrumentally than M, who was more prone to "label, imitate, and practice words" (p. 628). Input for the two children was, to some extent, different. M's mother "set up routines in which she would pick up an item, label it, and encourage her daughter to imitate it" (p. 627). "J and his mother did not participate in word-learning routines" (p. 628). Dore suggests that "there may be two partly separate lines of development—word development versus prosodic development" (p. 628). The diagram below depicts parallels in terminology among Peters, Nelson, and Dore.

Analytic language	Gestalt language

—"One word at a time" development
—Referential, labelling functions
   at first
—Clear mother-ese
	—Whole utterances in conversational
	   contexts
	—Rapid, conversational input

"Analytic": Peters "Referential": Nelson "Word development": Dore	"Gestalt": Peters "Expressive": Nelson "Prosodic development": Dore

Peters suggests that gestalt users may "have to convert slowly and painfully to a more analytic approach to language" (p. 13), holding that "creative language" (analytic language) eventually predominates. This is most consistent with position 2: gestalt language, which involves the heavy use of routines and patterns, may be a temporary strategy for the performer to outperform his analytic competence, to solve certain communication problems that his creative language has not evolved far enough to handle. Yet, since automatic speech appears to have a more limited use in actual speech performance than propositional language, all performers must eventually come to generate creative utterances at some point in their language development.

Automatic Speech in Child Second Language Acquisition

The impression one gets from the literature on child second language acquisition is that the second language performer relies far more on routines and patterns than does the first language acquirer. As we shall see below, Hatch and Hakuta provide evidence and slightly different, although complementary, reasons for this phenomenon. Then we will examine a study by Wagner-Gough which supports position 2. After this, we will review what is easily the most thorough treatment of routines and patterns in the language acquisition literature, L. Fillmore's documentation of routines and patterns in five Spanish-speaking children acquiring English as a second language.

Hatch (1972) describes the case history of Paul, a 4-year-old acquirer of English as a second language (see also Huang, 1971; Huang and Hatch, 1978). Paul, a Chinese speaker, was exposed to English in an informal environment, interacting with American children in school and in the playground. He made early use of the gestalt style. During the first month, "it seemed as if Paul was learning by imitation. He might repeat the sentence immediately after the other person said it, or he might remember it and use it later in the appropriate situation" (p. 31). "Propositional" speech appeared in the second month and looked quite similar to the analytic speech one generally sees in descriptions of child first language acquisition. Some typically analytic sentences included

> This kite.
> Ball no.
> Paper this.
> Wash hand?

At the same time, Paul was using complex routines such as

> Get out of here.
> It's time to eat and drink,

which he had learned by imitation. Hatch's comment neatly summarizes the situation: "Quite clearly two separate and very distinct strategies were running side by side. After week 12 it became increasingly difficult to separate out imitations since Paul's rule stages moved so fast that he quickly caught up with the language as it was spoken by the children in the playground" (p. 31).

The picture Hatch describes for Paul resembles, in reverse, what one may see in recovery patterns in aphasia. Alajouanine (1956) notes that when propositional speech returns, "fixed phrases" may disappear. The automatic speech is immune to the ungrammaticality of the aphasic's developing language.

The relationship of analytic and gestalt speech in Paul is again that predicted by position 2: the two modes are independent and the analytic mode eventually predominates, with gestalt speech primarily serving only as a short-cut, a pragmatic tool to allow social interaction with a minimum of linguistic competence.

Hatch suggests a reason why second language acquirers may use more routines and patterns than first language acquirers. She emphasizes the second language performer's greater capacity to remember longer utterances: "The person (L2 acquirer) brings with him a great capacity to create language by rule formation. At the same time he is capable of storing, repeating, and remembering large chunks of language via imitation. He can repeat them for use in an appropriate situation. While he is still at the two-word stage in rule formation, he can recall and use longer imitated sentences" (p. 33).

In another case history, Hakuta (1974) reported on the linguistic development of Uguisu, a Japanese-speaking 5-year-old acquiring English as a second language in informal situations in the United States. Hakuta reports that he found evidence for "a strategy of learning on the surface structure level: learning through rote memorization of segments of speech without knowledge of the internal structure of those speech segments" (p. 287).

Hakuta's study is mostly concerned with patterns (as opposed to routines): "segments of sentences which operate in conjunction with a movable component, such as the insertion of a noun phrase or a verb phrase", and the evidence he provides for the existence of patterns in his corpus is quite similar to that provided by Brown (1973) in his discussion of Adam (see discussion above). For example, copula forms are judged to be patterns due to very high learning performance, or the lack of a learning curve. Uguisu produced forms like "This is _____" accurately from the outset, while learning curves for other items (like the progressive and auxiliary morphemes) were gradual. Also, Uguisu overgeneralized the use of patterns, using patterns like "These are _____" in singular contexts much of the time. Another example is the *do you* phrase used as a question marker. Uguisu produced sentences like:

> What do you doing, boy?

These forms gradually gave way to correctly inflected forms for *do*.

In discussing why the child second language acquirer may use routines and patterns more than the first language acquirer, Hakuta emphasizes the older child's greater need to communicate: ". . . in the case of the second language learner, we would expect that, with advanced semantic development and yet no form with which to express such thoughts, the need to learn the various linguistic structures of the target language is especially acute." Until the structure of the language is acquired, it is conceivable, Hakuta suggests, that "the learner will employ a strategy which 'tunes in' on regular, patterned segments of speech, and employs them without knowledge of their underlying structure, but with the knowledge as to which particular situations call for what patterns. They may be thought of as props which temporarily give support until a firmer foundation is built . . ." (p. 288).

Synthesizing both Hatch and Hakuta, one may conclude that the child second language acquirer has both an increased need and ability to use routines and patterns. The child second language performer is placed in peer and school situations that demand linguistic interaction before competence is attained the "slow way", and the older child's advanced short-term memory allows him to pick up and retain the necessary formulas to facilitate interaction.

Another study which examines the use of routines and patterns in child second language acquisition is that of Wagner-Gough, 1975, see also Wagner-Gough and Hatch, 1975). Wagner-Gough noted that her subject Homer relied heavily on routines and patterns to communicate and often incorporated them into his speech. This is similar to what Clark found in her study of Adam. Wagner-Gough hypothesizes that patterns do not directly evolve into creative rule-governed language: "It is quite clear that there is no transfer between some imitations and subsequent free speech patterns. For example, a learner may say 'My name is Homer' in one breath and 'He Fred' in another, the former being a memorized pattern and the latter the learner's own rule" (p. 71). Thus, Wagner-Gough supports position 2.

The most complete study of routines and patterns in child second language acquisition is L. Fillmore's doctoral dissertation (Fillmore, 1976), an exhaustive examination of the speech produced by five acquirers of English as a second language in an English-speaking kindergarten. Unlike Wagner-Gough, Fillmore comes out strongly for position 3:

> . . . the strategy of acquiring formulaic speech is central to the learning of language: indeed, it is this step that puts the learner in a position to perform the analysis which is prerequisite to acquisition. The formulas . . . constituted the linguistic material on which a large part of their (the children's) analytical activities could be carried out. . . . Once they were in the learner's repertory, they became familiar, and therefore could be compared with other utterances in the repertory as well as with those produced by other speakers (p. 640).

All the children studied by Fillmore used routines and patterns very early and very heavily: "The most striking similarity among the spontaneous speech records of the five children was the acquisition and use of formulaic expressions. All five quickly acquired repertoires of expression which they knew how to use more or less appropriately, and put them to immediate and frequent use" (p. 640). Including only the clearest cases of formulaic expressions, Fillmore calculated that their use ranged from 52 per cent to 100 per cent of the total number of utterances at the early stages, down to a low of 37 per cent in the most advanced performer at the end of the year. Two children, in fact, remained nearly completely dependent on routines and patterns even at the end of the year.

Routines and patterns evolved into creative language in a manner not unlike that reported by R. Clark (1974). Larger units were broken into smaller units, routines became patterns, and parts of patterns were "freed" to recombine with other parts of patterns. This break-up of routines and patterns provided the basis for syntax, while morphology appeared much later:

> In the development of productive structure, the children all seemed to be following the strategy of working the major constituents first and dealing with the grammatical details later. . . . The process of gradual analysis by which parts of formulas become freed from their original frames yields sentence patterns . . . in the process, some of the grammatical morphemes and processes are unnoticed and lost (p. 656).

Fillmore documents many cases of these processes, and the interested reader is urged to consult her forthcoming book. We present here only a single example. Nora, Fillmore's fastest language acquirer, had these two formulas:

(1) I wanna play wi' dese.
(2) I don' wanna do dese.

She then discovered that the constituents following *wanna* were interchangeable, and that she could say

(3) I don' wanna play dese
and
(4) I wanna do dese.

She thus acquired the patterns "I wanna VP" and "I don' wanna VP". "Play with NP" then became a "formulaic verb phrase unit" which could be used for other slots requiring VP, e.g. "Le's VP", as in:

(5) Le's play wi' that one.

This "formula-based analytical process . . . was repeated in case after case of the children's spontaneous data" (p. 645). "Rules" came about when all the constituents of a formula were "freed".

Why did these children follow such a route? This question can be subdivided into several smaller ones. First, one may ask why so many routines and patterns occurred. Fillmore points out that the linguistic environment of the classroom and playground was conducive to the learning of routines and patterns. The daily classroom routine, for example, allowed the acquirers to figure out what was being said easily—all teachers followed, to a larger extent, predictable routines. "Such language, because it is used daily and with only minor variation, becomes highly predictable. The children can figure out

what utterances mean by observing how they relate to activities, and by noticing what their classmates do in response" (p. 637). The children thus rapidly acquired classroom expressions which were used daily ("It's time to clean up", "Finish your milk"). Playground games also have predictable language components that can be picked up rapidly.

Combined with this sort of environment, Fillmore also points out, as did Hakuta earlier, her subjects' needs to immediately establish social contact via language:

> . . . the desire to maintain contact and sustain social relations with members of the group is the motivation for the acquisition of formulaic speech.

Further,

> . . . what he (the acquirer) must do is to acquire some language which will give the impression of ability to speak it, so that his friends will keep trying to communicate with him. The use of formulas by the learners in this study played an important part in their being able to play with English speakers as they did. . . . This kind of language was extremely important, because it permitted the learners to continue participating in activities which provided contexts for the learning of new material (p. 670).

In other words, Fillmore's subjects were under great pressure to produce early and get along in the classroom and playground. Their use of routines and patterns was due to the fact that their communicative needs exceeded their linguistic competence, and they were forced to make the most of what they had. This resulted in the tremendous use of routines and patterns observed: "The children managed to get by with as little English as they did because they made the greatest use of what they had learned—and in the early part of the acquisition period, what they had learned was largely formulaic" (p. 654).

A second question is whether this is the way language is generally acquired. Clearly, the sort of early output demands Fillmore's subjects had imposed on them and the routinized predictable input are not present in most language acquisition situations. As we have seen in first language and second language acquisition by children, the "gestalt" route is used by acquirers under similar conditions: where input is complex, and where conversational demands are present, acquirers may tend to use whole utterances in conversationally appropriate places without a full grasp of their internal structure. The situation Fillmore describes certainly appears to be a clear case of this.

According to Fillmore, her children did get some "mother-ese" from their playmates, who did many things that fit the description of parental modification of language described for child L1 acquisition and informal child L2 acquisition (Clark and Clark, 1977; Brown and Hanlon, 1970; Wagner-Gough and Hatch, 1975). However, the overall input to these children may have been very complex, more so than the analytic acquirer usually gets. They were also faced with classroom input and much child input that, at least at first, they could not understand.

Fillmore's analysis shows clearly that under certain conditions the "gestalt" mode may be encouraged to a remarkable degree. It does not demonstrate that all language is acquired this way by all acquirers or even that the analytic style may be totally circumvented.

Routines and Patterns in Adult Second Language Acquisition

The use of routines and patterns is reported in only one adult study to our knowledge. (This rarity is undoubtedly due more to the paucity of data on adult second language acquisition than to the lack of automatic speech in adult second language performance.) Hanania and Gradman (1977) studied the English development of Fatmah, a 19-year-old Arabic speaker living in the United States. Fatmah had little formal schooling in Arabic and encountered English "primarily in natural communicative settings" (p. 76). Hanania and Gradman report that at the start of their study, Fatmah's English output "consisted mainly of memorized items that are commonly used in social contexts with children". They also noted that "the use of these expressions, however, does not imply that she recognized the individual words within them, or that she was able to use the words in new combinations. They were merely strings of sounds that she used appropriately in particular situations" (p. 78). In other words, she knew routines.

Fatmah also used patterns in the early stages: "An attempt was made to find out if Fatmah recognized units with sentences and could use them in new combinations, but such activity was apparently alien to her learning strategies. Structures like *Thank you, I can't . . ., Do you like . . .?*, were perceived as single units, and she resisted segmentation. Furthermore, she associated strings with particular situations. For instance, *See you* meant 'I'll be seeing you,' and it was used on occasions when her friends were parting. Attempts to lead her to combine it with *I can* to form *I can see you* were not only unsuccessful but confusing" (p. 79).

Ordinary analytic style grammatical development began subsequently. Hanania and Gradman report a slow development of sentence structure and morphology not at all unlike that seen in child first and second language acquisition: "Starting with simple structures made up of essential substantive units, she proceeded to build up her constructions by enlarging these units and linking them together. . . ." (p. 82). Hanania and Gradman's summary statement concerning Fatmah's syntactic development is also worth repeating:

> The adult in the present study proceeded to learn the language creatively. She did not simply imitate models of the language but acquired elements selectively and built them into syntactic units which became progressively more complex. The pattern of her linguistic development was similar to that of first language learners. Early constructions were constrained to two-term utterances, and the growth of sentence complexity occurred along the same lines (pp. 87–88).

The similarity of natural adult language acquisition has been noted elsewhere in terms of the acquisition order of certain structures (see Bailey, Madden, and Krashen, 1974; and also Krashen, 1977a).

While Hanania and Gradman do not note the disappearance or reanalysis of routines and patterns in Fatmah's speech, propositional language appears to be independent of gestalt in her case, as in Brown and Wagner-Gough's subjects and in Paul, the child L2 acquirer discussed above. Language development appears to proceed analytically, in the "one word at a time" fashion, and routines and patterns are not mentioned after the early stages. (We are presupposing that the "gestalt" mode is available to both the child and the adult. It is possible, however, that this mode is manifested somewhat differently for these two classes of acquirers: the child L1 acquirer, as Peters notes, sometimes approximates whole sentences which are characterized by "a 'melody' unique enough so that it can be recognized even if badly mumbled" (Peters, 1977, p. 562). The adult may use routines and patterns, but not "tunes". This child–adult difference may have a psychological-affective basis (see Krashen, 1980a).)

Other than Hanania and Gradman's study, there are no direct data on actual use of routines and patterns in adult second language performance. There is, however, some interesting literature from scholars concerned with materials and language pedagogy. Consider the "standard" audio-lingual technique of first memorizing a dialogue (as a routine) and then working on pattern practice. This is an implicit version of position 1: the routine is acquired from the dialogue and then broken into patterns for pattern practice, and it is suggested that the adult gains fluency through the use or transfer of these patterns to real conversational contexts. In other words, routines and patterns constitute all of language performance. (This is certainly not the view of all those scholars who encourage the use of pattern practice; see, for example, Rivers, 1972, pp. 10–12.)

To be sure, audio-lingual language teaching does result in increased student proficiency in second language, although other systems seem to be more efficient (see von Elek and Oskarsson, 1973). Does this mean that position 1 is correct? Not necessarily. It may appear to be the case that routines and patterns are being learned in the classroom and used as such in performance. In reality, proficiency gained in such circumstances is more likely due to the creative construction process, which is present in both adults and children (Krashen, 1977b), as well as the learning of explicit conscious rules (hypothesized to be used only as a Monitor).

First, even meaningless pattern practice may provide some, if less than optimal, input for the creative construction process. Second, such practice may also provide a domain for conscious rule learning, either as an environment for working out rules (inductive) or as a place to practice rule application (deductive) and to receive feedback.

The use of routines and patterns is certainly a part of language, but it is probably not a large part. In fact, many second language performers report that it is often quite difficult to find a spot in a conversation for a routine or pattern learned in a dialogue (K. Schule, personal communication). In addition, sometimes performers report having to run through an entire dialogue to get to the appropriate line!

Even if the gestalt mode *per se* were learned in the audiolingual class, there are dangers in encouraging adults to use it. The outside world for adults is nowhere near as predictable as the linguistic environment around Fillmore's children was. The wide use of routines and patterns other than as discourse conventions (such as greetings and attention-getters) and in limited contexts (for example, commercial and sports domains) encourages very complex input that may be useless to the performer or that may place him in an awkward situation. Consider what often happens when the traveller attempts to use his phrase book to ask "Where is the opera?" The answer may be a barrage of incomprehensible input, for example, "You go two blocks until you see a big church, then turn left until you come to a traffic light. . . ." Use of strategies such as employing yes/no questions instead of WH-questions may alleviate this problem. Still, responses to adult routines and patterns may be highly unpredictable and complex.

Conclusions

The available evidence indicates that routines and patterns are essentially and fundamentally different from creative language. Most studies support the correctness of position 2, that the creative construction process is independent of routines and patterns. It appears to be the case, however, that the use of the gestalt mode is possible and may be encouraged by certain environmental conditions. This alternative route may be the acquirer's reaction to demands for early production before sufficient competency has been built up. Routines and patterns may be very useful for establishing social relations and encouraging intake. They could conceivably serve as intake for the creative construction process. This intake, however, is probably insufficient for successful language acquisition. Adult teaching systems, such as the audio-lingual, seem to imply that positions 1 or 3 are correct. But these systems enjoy the limited success they do because they also provide at least some intake for the creative construction process. More successful teaching systems expose second language acquirers to input in which routines and patterns play a minor, though significant role.

8. Relating Theory and Practice in Adult Second Language Acquisition

Applications

In this chapter we will attempt to make the difficult transition from theory to practice. This will be done by describing what appears to me to be an "ideal" second language teaching program in general terms. The program contains several components, some of which are obligatory and some of which are optional.

Most language teaching programs, if they are subdivided into components, divide up into the "four skills", speaking, listening, reading, and writing. Evidence from a variety of sources indicates that this may not be the optimal division. First, in every program I have been associated with, teachers who are asked to focus on just one of the four skills, or even two (oral versus written), complain that such divisions are artificial. They find it impossible to focus on just one skill and ignore the others. Second, Oller, in a series of studies, reports that "it is difficult to find any unique meaningful variance in all of the diverse language tests that have been studied and which can be attributed to any one of the traditionally recognized four skills" (Oller, 1976a, p. 144; see also Oller, 1976b; Oller and Hinofotis, 1976). In other words, there is no clear evidence for a "reading" factor, a "speaking" factor, etc. Also, there is no evidence for an oral modality factor, as opposed to a written modality factor. Our research on "Monitor Theory" is also consistent with the idea that the four skills are not the primary division: Oller (1976a) has noted that error analysis "reveals a high degree of correspondence between the structures generated in widely different tasks, e.g. translation, oral imitation, and spontaneous speech" (p. 144). While this generalization is based on data gathered before "Monitor" research was reported, our results have been quite consistent with this generalization. We find similar difficulty orders for grammatical morphemes produced by adult second language performers in "widely different tasks", as described above, tasks whose commonality is that they tap the acquired, rather than the learned system.

The theoretical model thus implies that the language teaching program will have two major components, acquisition and learning, which occupy the "NP" and "VP" nodes in Fig. 1.

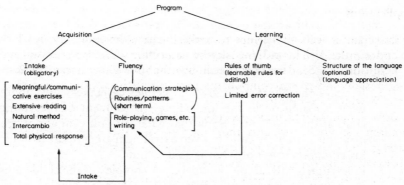

Fig. 1. A second language teaching program

Acquisition

The theoretical model clearly implies that the most important part of the entire program is the intake node under the "acquisition" node, in Fig. 1. This follows from our conclusions that language acquisition is more central than language learning in second language perform-ance. "Intake" is, simply, where language acquisition comes from, that subset of linguistic input that helps the acquirer acquire language. It appears to be the case to me now that *the major function of the second language classroom is to provide intake for acquisition.* This being a very difficult task, one could also say that the major challenge facing the field of applied linguistics is to create materials and contexts that provide intake.

In another paper (Krashen, 1978b), I attempted to define intake, and I will very briefly review this definition and the evidence that led to it. I made the assumption, one that others have made, that "caretaker" speech, language addressed to young children acquiring their first language, contained a high proportion of *intake*, and suggested that by examining the essential properties of caretaker speech we could arrive at some definition of intake. As many researchers have pointed out (Snow and Ferguson, 1977), caretakers do not consciously intend to teach language; their concern is communication. Nevertheless, there is reason to suppose that caretaker speech is an excellent teaching language, even though it may not always seem to be at first examination. According to the literature on caretaker speech (my primary sources include the summary in Clark and Clark, 1977, and the superb collection edited by Snow and Ferguson, 1977), caretaker speech has the following characteristics:

1. It obeys the "here and now" principle: caretakers talk about what is going on in the immediate environment of the young child at that moment. I think that what is significant about this principle is that the child is given extralinguistic support to aid in his *comprehension* of what is said to him.
2. It is syntactically simple, and becomes complex as the child gains in linguistic maturity. This characteristic is not as simple as that, however. Caretakers do not simply aim their input at the "next" structure, the one that the child is due to acquire next. Rather, caretaker input appears to be "roughly tuned" to the child's linguistic ability—we see positive, but not strikingly high correlations between linguistic input complexity and linguistic competence in children (Newport, Gleitman, and Gleitman, 1977; Cross, 1977; Chapter 9, this volume).
3. Caretaker speech is communication. As mentioned above, the purpose of caretaker speech is not language teaching, it is to convey messages and often to get the child to behave in a certain way. It turns out to be the case that caretaker speech is effective in encouraging language acquisition (at least the literature is consistent with this view; Cross, 1977; Newport *et al.*, 1977).

From these characteristics, it can be hypothesized that intake is first of all input that is *understood*. Indeed, comprehension may be at the heart of the language acquisition process: perhaps we acquire by *understanding* language that is "a little beyond" our current level of competence. This is done with the aid of extra-linguistic context or our knowledge of the world. (In more formal terms, if an acquirer is at stage i in acquisition of syntax, he can progress to stage $i+1$ by understanding input at that level of complexity.)

It follows from this that optimal input includes structures that are "just beyond" the acquirer's current level of competence, and that it tends to get progressively more complex. This progression, however, need not be exactly matched to the acquirer's developing competence: "rough tuning" may be optimal. Simply aiming for $i+1$ may be less efficient, as one's aim may miss, less review is provided, and where there is variation in rate of acquisition, fewer acquirers may be accommodated by the same input (for detailed discussion, see Chapter 9). It also follows that intake is "natural", which means that it is language used for communication.

One can easily analyze various second language classroom activities to see to what extent they provide optimal input, as described above. Simple "free conversation" will often fail as optimal input, as it is often not understood. The failure of free conversation to qualify as intake implies that second language teaching involves more than just talking to students about topics of interest, something the profession has known since its beginning. Administrators, however, sometimes feel that being a native speaker of a language qualifies one to be a teacher of that language. This analysis shows why this is not necessarily true.

Mechanical drill also fails as optimal intake for acquisition. Mechanical drill is activity in which the primary focus is on the *form* of the language being used rather than its communicative intent. Here is a sample: given the sentence "John is a student", change it to the negative ("John isn't a student"). Whether anyone is interested in the fact that John is or is not a student is, of course, not an issue. Thus, while mechanical drills may be understood, they are understood only in a trivial sense. Evidence (Lee, McCune, and Patton, 1970) is available that suggests strongly that students do not pay much attention to repetitive drill after a few repetitions, and it is doubtful that the meaning strikes very "deeply" (in the sense of Stevick, 1976). Mechanical drills are, of course, not natural, nor are they intended to be. Thus, mechanical drills are at best only partially suitable for acquisition. Together with free conversation (the "structure" and the "conversation" class combination), they may succeed in encouraging some language acquisition, but I think the second language classroom can do much better.

My analysis of what intake is predicts that what is called "meaningful" and "communicative" drills or exercises can be more efficient in producing language acquisition. These are activities in which students can really communicate or in which communication can be simulated. My impression is that designing materials for mechanical practice is not difficult. Nor is it difficult to think of things to talk about in class. Providing intake via meaningful and communicative activities is quite a challenging task, however. In order to qualify as intake, these exercises must be understood, be at the appropriate level, and be "natural". I have tried to come up with activities that fit these requirements as an ESL teacher, and I found it very difficult to think up interesting, natural communicative situations in which to contextualize "the structure of the day".

I have also been struck by the popularity of presentations at language teaching conferences and workshops that give teachers ideas for contextualization of structure. Such presentations are well attended and eagerly received. One rarely sees, these days, demonstrations of new mechanical drills. I interpret this trend as the recognition of the fact that language acquisition develops better when the intake is communicative and understood.

Even meaningful and communicative drills may have their limitations, however. Even if they manage to hit the "next" structure ($i + 1$), which is unlikely for all students in a given class, they may fail to provide enough input or be natural enough for language acquisition. Perhaps the correct generalization is that the best activities are those that are natural, interesting, and understood. When these requirements are met, and where there is a great deal of input of this nature, it may be the case that $i + 1$ will "naturally" be covered and reviewed many times over, and progress in language acquisition will result.

If intake does indeed have these characteristics, and if intake is the most essential part of the language teaching program, the classroom may, in fact, be the best place for adults to acquire language, at least up to the intermediate level. As Wagner-Gough and Hatch (1975) have pointed out, the "outside world" is usually unwilling to provide the adult with intake. Children acquiring second languages often do have the advantage of receiving real intake, but adults may not. Consider this conversation between a 5-year-old ESL acquirer and an adult:

Adult	Paul
Is this your ball?	Yeah.
What colour is your ball?	(no answer)
Is that your doggy?	Yeah.
Is that your doggy or Jim's doggy?	Jim's doggy.

(Huang, cited in Wagner-Gough, 1975)

In this exchange, the requirements for intake are clearly met. Paul's responses indicate that he understands much if not all of the speech directed at him (thanks, perhaps, to the adult's adherence to the "here and now" principle), it is simple input, most likely at or near the level Paul needs in order to acquire more English, and it is quite natural. Compare this to the input that the older acquirer needs to deal with. As Wagner-Gough and Hatch point out, the language is quite complex, displaced in time and space, and probably incomprehensible to acquirers such as Ricardo, a 13-year-old acquirer of English as a second language:

Adult	Ricardo
What are you gonna do tonight?	Tonight? I don't know.
You don't know yet? Do you work at home, do the dishes or sweep the floor?	Water . . .
Flowers.	Mud.
Oh. You wash the mud down and all that. What else do you do at home?	Home.

(Butterworth, 1972; cited in Wagner-Gough, 1975)

Despite this sort of behavior from native speakers, there may be useful sources of intake outside the classroom. One resource is the foreign student peer group. The language our ESL students direct at each other may come quite close to meeting the requirements for intake. Their communication with each other is certainly natural and usually understood, and the presence of peers who are slightly more advanced provides, often, for input that is "just beyond" the acquirer's current level. While it may seem to be the case that foreign students will acquire each others' errors, this may not be a serious problem, as "error-free" intake sources will also be available (native Speakers both inside and outside the classroom). Fathman (1976) presents evidence suggesting that the presence of a foreign student peer group may in fact be beneficial. In her study of ESL students in elementary schools in the Washington, D.C. area, she found that "the students in schools where there were more than forty non-native English speakers seemed to make more progress than those in schools where there were fewer foreign sudents" (p. 437). This may be due, Fathman points out, to the fact that schools that had more foreign students tended to have better-organized school programs for them. However, "the students within these groups became friends with those from other countries with whom they spoke English" (p. 438). Helping foreign students get to know each other has always been a popular activity in ESL classes (V. Sferlazza, personal communication); it may be linguistically justified, and should perhaps be encouraged as good pedagogy.

In a recent paper, I suggest another way of obtaining intake outside the classroom, a way of encouraging the outside world to cooperate with the language teaching profession (Krashen, 1978e): "Language Learning Buttons" would alert native speakers to the linguistic needs of acquirers—a red button, designated "ESL Learner 1" would mean a beginning ESL student, a yellow button designated "ESL Learner 2" an intermediate, etc. Native speakers would hopefully provide the bearer of such a button with simpler input (and perhaps a friendlier response).

Returning to the classroom, in recent years some novel ideas have been suggested that encourage language acquisition by providing intake. Terrell (1977) has proposed a method which he calls the "Natural Approach", in which class time essentially consists of communicative activity, with the teacher speaking only in the target language, and the students responding in either the target language or their first language. Students' errors are completely ignored during this activity, unless there is some communication failure. Homework is of the usual sort, grammar exercises, etc. Of course, such a system is practical only in a foreign language situation, where the teacher is also a speaker of the (one) student native language, but it does give the possibility for massive amounts of intake. A USC graduate student, John Cromshaw, has also come up with an interesting innovation which he calls "Intercambio". In intercambio, as it is practiced at USC, Americans studying Spanish as a foreign language are teamed with Spanish-speaking ESL students, and are encouraged to converse on various topics. The rule is: speak your own language! Cromshaw reports that even less advanced students exchange enormous amounts of information with each other, and often, involuntarily, begin to speak in the target language. These approaches have been validated only informally, but early reports of their success have been quite encouraging.

Several other activities, better known to the profession, may also fit the requirements for intake: extensive reading, as recommended by Newmark (1971), will certainly provide more intake than the difficult paragraphs that require cryptoanalytic decoding that we sometimes assign second language students. Also, the use of techniques such as Asher's "total physical response" (Asher, 1966, 1969) may also provide useful amounts of intake in the classroom. In Asher's approach, students remain silent in early stages, but are required to obey teacher commands in the target language, commands that require a "total physical response", beginning with simple imperatives ("sit down") to more complex sentences ("If John ran to the blackboard, run after him and hit him with your book"). There is some experimental evidence in Asher's papers that "TPR" does indeed work: foreign language students, after 32 hours of TPR, had significantly better listening comprehension scores than students in "ordinary" classes after 150 hours, and scores on other tests were about the same. Clearly, teacher input that stimulates a total physical response will be close if not totally intake: it is understood, at an appropriate level, and natural, its goal being communication.

Before leaving the intake node of the "program tree", several points need clarification. First, I have posited that *intake* is fundamental to acquisition, and have not mentioned what function *output* may play. It may be argued that *theoretically* speaking and writing are not essential to acquisition. One can acquire "competence" in a second language, or a first language, without ever producing it. There are several supporting arguments for this *intake hypothesis*.

First, as mentioned earlier, there are several studies showing that delaying speech in second language instruction, when active listening is provided, causes no delay in attaining proficiency in second language acquisition, and may even be beneficial (for child second language acquisition see Gary, 1975; for adult studies see Asher, 1965, 1966, 1969; Postovsky, 1977). Also, there are suggestive informal accounts of language acquisition in other cultures, where active listening is stressed. Here is Sorenson's (1967) report on the American Indians in the Vaupes River area:

> The Indians do not practice speaking a language they do not know well yet. Instead, they passively learn lists of words, forms, phrases in it and familiarize themselves with the sound of its pronunciation . . . They may make an occasional attempt to speak a new language in an appropriate situation, but if it does not come easily, they will not force it.

Finally, there is the well-established fact from child language acquisition studies that comprehension normally precedes production. Production, in fact, need never occur. Lenneberg (1962) describes a case of congenital dysarthria in an 8-year-old boy who never spoke, but who could understand spoken English perfectly well. Lenneberg noted that:

> (A) similar phenomenon in more attenuated form is extremely common. Understanding normally precedes speaking by several weeks or months. This discrepancy is regularly increased in literally all types of developmental speech disorders and is best illustrated in children who have structural deformities in the oral cavity or pharynx and who produce unintelligible speech for years—sometimes throughout life—without the slightest impairment of understanding. Congenitally deaf children also learn to comprehend language in the absence of vocal skills. . . . However, there is no clear evidence that speaking is ever present in the absence of understanding.

This does not mean that speaking is not of practical importance, and it may be the case that speaking may indirectly promote language acquisition. What may be the case is that speaking, engaging in conversation, encourages intake. "Eavesdropping" (Schumann and Schumann, 1977) may provide the acquirer with a certain amount of intake, but actual conversation, in which the acquirer has at least some control of the topic and in which the acquirer's conversational partner is making some effort at making himself understood, may provide more intake.

We return to the role of output below.

Another point that deserves mention in discussion of intake is the role of vocabulary. The view of the profession has been to restrict vocabulary in order to focus on syntax: we were told that language is not words, but is grammar. My view is just the opposite: emphasize vocabulary in order to encourage the acquisition of syntax. Recall that a primary characteristic of intake is that it is understood, and that the child acquirer often has the benefit of participating in conversations that focus on the "here and now", which provides extra-linguistic support that facilitates comprehension. Adults, however, since they usually talk about ideas displaced in time and space, need some other means of extra-linguistic support: this can, at least in part, be provided by vocabulary. Knowing the words, even without knowing the syntax, provides the listener with enough information so that a great deal can be understood. With comprehension, my model predicts, acquisition of syntax will come. Hatch (1978) makes a very similar point, and notes that "adult second language learners have been telling us that (vocabulary is important) for years (and perhaps it's time we listened to their intuitions of what would help them in language classes)" (p. 430). I have no position as to how vocabulary should be taught or how many words are necessary to be taught per day, nor do I know of any compelling experimental literature that supports any method of vocabulary teaching over another. But it does seem to be very important.

The third point I need to mention before moving on to other parts of the program is the most important. I place it last and give it less salience in this chapter only because it has been discussed elsewhere in detail (Chapter 2, this volume) and very eloquently and clearly in Stevick's *Memory, Meaning, and Method*: this is the issue of motivation and attitude. In Chapter 2 it was noted that aspects of motivation and attitude that appear to relate to second language proficiency appear to relate more directly to acquisition than to learning. Again, the detailed argumentation appears elsewhere, and need not be repeated here. What is worth repeating, however, is how this finding relates to practice. Dulay and Burt (1977) have suggested that an "affective filter" may exist, a filter that "delimits" input before it can be processed by the "cognitive organizer". In our terms, some potential intake may not make it to the "language acquisition device": acquirers' motivations and attitudes, if they are less than optimal, may filter out certain aspects of the input, so that they are no longer available to the acquirer as intake, even if the requirements for intake outlined above are met. Thus, motivational and attitudinal considerations are *prior* to linguistic considerations. If the affective filter is "up", no matter how beautifully the input is sequenced, no matter how meaningful and communicative the exercise is intended to be, little or no acquisition will take place. Again, I refer the reader to Chapter 2 of this volume for detailed discussion of those aspects of attitude that have been found to be related to language acquisition.

Figure 2 illustrates the relationship between attitude and motivation

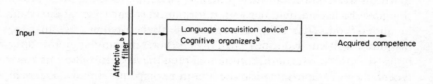

Adapted from Chomsky, 1964[a]; Dulay and Burt, 1977[b]

Fig. 2. The relationship between affective factors and language acquisition

and language acquisition. It clearly implies that attitude and motivation are of central importance, a fact that most language teachers seem to be aware of already.

The second node under the "acquisition" node of the tree is labelled "fluency". While intake builds acquisition, some fluency work may be necessary to enable the performer to perform this competence in a workable way. To what extent this is to be done depends, of course, on the situation. In foreign language acquisition (e.g. French in the United States), it probably does not pay to emphasize this aspect of the program, as students will not need to perform in French in their everyday life. In second language programs (e.g. ESL) there is a real need for early and functional second language production, and the program needs to deal with this need.

It may be useful to distinguish three distinct ways in which second language production may be performed. First, a performer may simply utilize his acquired system to initiate utterances. Normally, performance using the acquired system does not emerge right away. As mentioned above, comprehension precedes production: children acquiring second languages typically exhibit a "silent period" during which acquired competence is built up via active listening, via intake (Chapter 5, this volume); this period may last several months. Performers have two alternative means for outperforming their acquired competence, however. One is the use of prefabricated patterns and routines, sentences that are memorized wholes (routines such as "What's your name?", "How are you?") or partially memorized wholes (patterns with an open "slot" for a word or phrase, such as "Down with _____" or "That's a _____"). The use of routines and patterns may be of immense practical value. Performers in a second language situation may need to say things very early on, before their acquired competence is "ready" to produce sentences using the acquired system. Routines such as "Where is the _____?", "My _____ hurts", etc., are commonly taught early for good reason. Scarcella and I have reviewed the literature on routines and patterns in language acquisition and neurolinguistics, and conclude that the development of patterns and routines is a process that is quite independent of "normal" language acquisition (Chapter 6, this volume). *Theoretically*, routines and patterns do not contribute much to language acquisition, but practically, they may help quite a bit.[1]

A third way to produce utterances in a second language is to rely on the surface structure of the first language, and to attempt to make changes/corrections using the conscious grammar, the Monitor. According to Newmark (1966), the second language performer may "fall back" on his first language when he wishes to produce an utterance but has not acquired enough of the second language to do so. In terms of the Monitor Model, the performer uses the first language as a substitute utterance initiator. My review of the available literature on the effect of the first language on second language performance (Chapter 5) supports Newmark's idea—we see first language influence just where and when it would be expected, in structures that tend to be acquired rather than learned, and in situations in which early production is valued and in which acquisition opportunities are lacking—foreign language learning situations. Also, first language influence errors seem to give way over time (Taylor, 1975). Using the first language, like the use of routines and patterns, is thus a way of performing without acquired competence. While both of these methods are "unnatural", in a sense, when students are in a situation where early production is absolutely necessary, one certainly cannot object to the use of this mode.

The use of routines and patterns, and the use of the first language as a substitute utterance initiator, while useful in early production emergency situations, have real disadvantages for long-term utilization. Effective use of routines and patterns depends on having a "line" ready when a situation arises. The situation may not come up, or worse yet, you may not have a line for every situation. Also, a well-formed, appropriate question may encourage input that is far beyond the performer's ability to understand: a beginner asking "Where is the museum?" may get quite an involved answer (using a yes/no question might be a better strategy). Relying on the use of the first language to initiate utterances is also limited: elsewhere I have argued that the Monitor is fairly limited with respect to what sorts of "repairs" it can perform—it does fairly well with simple, bound morphology, but has a difficult time with more complex rules, such as those involving word order changes or subtle semantic rules. Since it is up to the Monitor to make the utterance conform to the second language surface structure, this may be a forbidding task where the two languages differ in more than bound morphology. Also, as mentioned earlier, Monitor use is highly restricted for most people.

What can be done in the fluency section? While the student speech produced will have some effect on acquisition of fellow students (see discussion above on the "foreign student peer group"), the main goal of the fluency section, as I see it, is to aid in performance. The rapid acquisition of essential routines and patterns for performers who need them, help in appropriate word choice, and practice in the use of communication strategies (avoidance of structures that have not yet been acquired may be important goals for students in a second language situation where early production is important). Such a section is less important for foreign language students, who can enjoy the luxury of building up acquired competence through an extended silent period, without early speaking demands.

Learning

The "program tree" contains two lower nodes under the "learning" node, one for rules that may be used by the optimal user for editing, and one for more difficult rules that some students may enjoy learning about. As I have pointed out in previous papers, there is no necessity of providing any conscious learning in the "acquisition" section of the tree. Despite the (completely untested) claims of the "cognitive code" method, there is no evidence to support the claim that conscious learning needs to precede acquisition (Krashen, 1977a). We see performers who have known a (late-acquired) rule for years, but who still fail to consistently "get it right" even after thousands of repetitions. Such performers may have acquired a great deal of English but have simply not yet acquired all of it, and there remain some late-acquired items "to go". For example, our subject "P", in Krashen and Pon (1975), even after many years in the US and with her extensive formal knowledge of English grammar, still occasionally made mistakes with the third person singular morpheme for regular verbs in the present tense. These errors were in casual speech: in writing she was able to use her conscious grammar and make the necessary correction. This morpheme happens to be one that is generally acquired late in second language acquisition (Bailey, Madden, and Krashen, 1974), and it is quite predictable that it be an item that is resistant to acquisition.[2]

On the other hand, we often see performers who have acquired large amounts of a second language with no apparent conscious learning. Monitor "underusers" described in the literature (Stafford and Covitt, 1978; Chapter 1, this volume; Kounin and Krashen, 1978) are typically able to use surprisingly difficult structures and have no idea as to their formal description.

There is no denying that there is a certain satisfaction, for some of us, in knowing a conscious rule, and I believe that this feeling may be some of the motivation for insisting that conscious rules always precede performance—but it is important to point out that insisting on conscious rules first constrains what can be taught. Linguists readily admit that they can describe only fragments of natural language. Second language textbooks and teachers can probably convert only a subset of the linguists' descriptions into clear pedagogical rules, and our students probably understand only a subset of that. If we insist on conscious control preceding acquisition, only a small fraction of language will be acquired. This fact is probably the reason why there is such a dearth of second-year foreign language textbooks, and such an abundance of first-year books. The first-year books encourage the conscious learning of easy rules, or those rules which can be learned by most college freshmen. The second-year books attempt to deal with the difficult rules, the subjunctive, contrary-to-fact conditionals, etc. According to my model, these second-year rules, if they are mastered, are acquired, and only the most analytic and able students learn them. Materials encouraging their acquisition, I predict, will be far more successful than materials encouraging their learning.

The "learning node" dominates two subnodes, one labelled "rules of thumb" and the other "structure of the target language". The former is learning that is actually meant as an aid to performance, the latter is optional learning, or language appreciation. "Rules of thumb" are those rules which the optimal user can apply to performance, conscious rules for the Monitor. It has been suggested (Krashen, Butler, Birnbaum, and Robertson, 1978) these rules are those that are (1) late acquired (or better, not yet acquired), and (2) "easy" to learn. "Easy" can be defined in two ways: first, not involving extensive mental gymnastics. A rule requiring a great deal of movement and permutation will not be easy to learn and apply. Examples might include the passive rule in English, or wh-questions in English. Another way in which a rule can be called "easy" is where the semantics of the rule are straightforward. Article use in English is simple in terms of the syntactic operations involved, but it is anything but "easy" in terms of the subtle semantic considerations required for its correct use. I am not prepared to supply a definite list of what rules can be taught; this is, I think, a worthy task for the Applied Linguistics profession to pursue. I can suggest a few examples, however. In syntax, the late, straightforward morphemes include the third person singular ending on regular verbs in the present tense, the possessive marker /-s/, and the regular and irregular past endings. In writing, easily learned and useful rules include punctuation (but not all aspects: rules for capitalization and quotation marks are straightforward, but the rules for the comma and semi-colon may need to be acquired), and some spelling rules. The use of rules of thumb can increase accuracy in monitored performance to some extent. They will probably not make a great deal of difference in terms of communicative effectiveness, as these late-acquired items tend to be fairly redundant, but they will give the performer's writing and prepared speech a more educated appearance (Kounin and Krashen, 1978).

The "structure of the language" node is an optional section for those who have a genuine interest in the linguistics of the target language. I would personally be very interested in such information in any language I was acquiring, and most language science professionals, I assume, would also be interested. My impression is that most of our students would not be as eager for this kind of information, and the position outlined here implies that they need not be in order to gain a high level of proficiency in the target language. It is this class that can be devoted to a transformational analysis of the language being acquired, where the historical development of the language can be traced, etc. Students in such an optional section may need to be told that this information is not meant for use in actual language performance, unless one is a "super Monitor user".[3]

While the components are listed separately on the tree, we might see some intercommunication between them: for example, *some* of the output of the "fluency" component might be a domain for error correction, as an aid to learning the rules of thumb. It makes sense to me that not all errors would be corrected: if error correction aims at changing the student's conscious mental representation of a rule, it follows that only those rules that are "learnable" need be corrected, only the rules of thumb. Also, as mentioned above, students' output in the fluency section provides intake for other students, as does teacher-talk in the formal "rules of thumb" section, at least in second language acquisition situations.

Conclusions

My major point in this paper is to suggest that the second language classroom might be a very good place for second language acquisition. The literature (Upshur, 1968; Carroll, 1967; Mason, 1971) contains some interesting evidence that the informal environment might be better than the classroom, but my re-analysis of these data indicates that what is really at issue is the amount of *intake* the acquirer can get (Chapter 3). In intake-rich informal environments, acquisition occurs, and in intake-poor classrooms, acquisition suffers. The acquisition-rich classroom might be extremely efficient, perhaps the most efficient solution for the adult second language acquirer.

There are several ways in which a classroom can promote language acquisition. Intake is available via meaningful and communicative activities supplied by the teacher; this is the most direct way the classroom can promote language acquisition. As we have seen, there are other ways in which the classroom can encourage acquisition: in second language situations, it can aid in the development of the foreign student peer group, which is quite possibly an important intermediate source of intake. What is considered the most essential component of language instruction, explicit information about the language, and mechanical drill, may be the least important contributions the second language classroom makes. Although I can certainly study grammar on my own, I would elect to attend a second language class if I were again abroad for some period of time in a country where I did not know the language; my intention would be to gain intake, from the teacher, the classroom exercises, and from my fellow students.

The subjects in the "Good Language Learner" study (Naimon, Fröhlich, Stern, and Todesco, 1978) (the 34 case histories in the first section) combined "grammar" study and "immersion" as their preferred approach to second language acquisition. Naimon *et al.* note that there is some evidence that ". . . those subjects who learned a language in the country of the target language, though frequently combined with self-study, usually acquired it successfully" (p. 34). On the other hand, grammar study by itself was not the answer. Several "good language learners" had grammar-type courses in the target language in school: ". . . in retrospect, several interviewees, who had achieved high marks in their language courses in school had attached little significance to this aspect of success . . . as they felt they were not able

to speak the language they were learning, or if so, only haltingly ..."
(p. 34). This evidence is consistent with the generalization that the
chief value of second language classes is their ability to provide the
acquirer with appropriate intake, a conclusion that language teachers,
through practice and experience, have come up with, and one which
"theory", in this case "theory of language acquisition", also supports.

Notes

[1] Especially important are routines that enable acquirers to "manage" conversations
with speakers who are more competent than they are in the language, routines that
allow acquirers to get speakers to slow down, interrupt when necessary, change the
subject, get help with vocabulary, etc.

[2] It often "looks like" learning causes acquisition. This occurs when a second language
acquirer has learned a rule before actually acquiring it, and then subsequently does
succeed in acquiring the rule. It may appear as if the learning led to the acquisition. I
am claiming that this is not the way the acquisition really occurred. A hypothetical
example may make this clear.

Consider the case of two ESL performers living in the United States, M and U. M is
a Monitor user, while U is not. They have acquired equal amounts of English and are
exposed to identical input/intake. Let us also assume that there does indeed exist an
"average" order of acquisition for grammatical items, as claimed in Chapter 4.
Figure 3 illustrates M's and U's progress along this natural order.

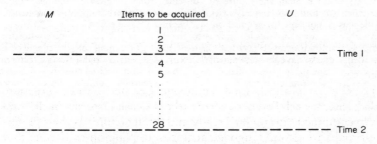

Fig. 3. Hypothetical case of two ESL acquirers.

At time 1, both M and U have acquired up to item 3. (This is, of course, a vast
oversimplification; there is some individual variation in order of acquisition, and it is
known that items are not acquired in a rigidly linear order. Also, acquisition is not
"all or none" as Brown (1973), Hakuta (1974), and Rosansky (1976) show;
acquisition is not sudden, and "acquisition curves" are not even necessarily linear.)
Item 28, far down the line, happens to be an item that is easily "learnable" (such as
the third person singular morpheme on regular verbs in English), and is typically
presented early in ESL classes. M, being a conscious learner, has no problem gaining

an explicit mental representation of 28, and begins to apply his conscious rule at time 1. He is thus able to supply rule 28 when the conditions for Monitor use are met: time and focus on form, and his performance on rule 28 is therefore variable. U ignored the formal presentation of 28 in class and does not supply it at all until time 2. At time 2, both M and U *acquire* 28, and use it consistently and appropriately in performance from time 2 on. This acquisition was due to the intake both M and U received up to time 2. (Again, I assume sudden and perfect acquisition, and the authors cited above have shown that this does not occur—acquisition curves are gradual and somewhat irregular. I ignore this source of variability in this example.)

Looking only at M, it appears to be the case that his conscious control of 28 was responsible for his automatic-like control of 28 at time 2. There is, however, another possibility—M's conscious use of 28 before time 2 may have had nothing to do with his subsequent acquisition of rule 28. Rather, 28 was acquired by both M and U through understanding intake, where the focus was on meaning and not form. (In a trivial sense, M's own use of 28 was intake, especially at the time M was "ready" for 28 and may have added to the intake from other sources.) The model I am proposing predicts, moreover, that U, dealing with the same intake, would acquire 28 at the same time as M (or maybe slightly later—see comments above). In the case of U, no conscious knowledge preceded acquired competence.

In a sense, M was "faking" 28 until his acquisition caught up, or until he arrived at rule 28 "naturally". Until time 2, he was outperforming his acquired competence.

Some performers will not make it to 28 at all; they will "fossilize" (Selinker, 1972) earlier, due to failure to obtain enough intake, or a failure to utilize intake for acquisition due to an overactive affective filter. The conscious rule may, in this case, be the permanent solution.

Positing a natural order and the existence of language acquisition in the adult allows us to explain the failure of conscious rules to always become automatic competence, and also explains cases like the above, where it appears that conscious rule was responsible for acquisition just because it "came first".

[3] Another use for conscious learning is to give Monitor overusers some confidence in the acquisition process. I have had the experience of teaching rules to advanced ESL students, and to have them comment "Oh yes, that's exactly right, that's exactly how it works". Such responses indicated to me that the students had already acquired the structure I was attempting to teach, but had not learned it until my lesson. Students are often very happy to get this knowledge and feel they have really learned something. The only benefit I can see that such teaching may give, aside from the "language appreciation" function, is that an occasional overuser may be brought to understand that subconscious language acquisition is indeed a reality, and that he or she has a great deal of acquired competence that is worthy of his or her trust.

9. The Theoretical and Practical Relevance of Simple Codes in Second Language Acquisition

One of the most interesting case histories in the second language acquisition literature deals with two young acquirers of English as a second language, one successful and one unsuccessful. Paul, the successful acquirer, was 5 years old when he was first studied by E. Hatch's student, Huang (1971). According to Wagner-Gough and Hatch (1975), at least some of Paul's progress can be attributed to the fact that he had the benefit of input that was more appropriate for language acquisition. He engaged in conversations such as this one:

Adult	Paul
Paul, are you writing?	Yeah.
What are you doing?	I'm write.
Paul, are you writing?	Yeah.
What are you doing?	I'm writing.
Is the baby crying?	Baby is crying.

Such simple input is fixed on the "here and now" and contains a "limited body of graded language data", according to Wagner-Gough and Hatch.

Ricardo, the unsuccessful acquirer, was 13 years old when he was studied by Butterworth (1972), another student of Hatch. Despite the fact that Ricardo had been in the United States only a few months, he had to participate in discussions that were quite complex, involving topics displaced in time and space and often using advanced syntactical constructions. Here is an example:

Adult	Ricardo
In Columbia, do they (lobsters) have claws?	Claws?
Claws. Do they have . . . the lobsters do they have claws?	Octopus?
No. The lobsters. Do the lobsters have hands?	Huh?

Questions asked Ricardo during the first few months of his stay in the United States included:

What do we mean by question mark?
Did you ever have any trouble with your ears?

Wagner-Gough and Hatch suggest that it was this input difference, rather than the age difference between Paul and Ricardo, that was the fundamental reason for their differential success in acquiring English as a second language.

What could we have done for Ricardo? I can think of at least three ways Ricardo could have been provided with simpler input in English. First, he could have been a member of a "pull-out" class in school, either in English as a second language or in one or more subject-matters. This segregation from native speakers of English, distasteful to some, would have at least encouraged a simpler "teacher-talk" from his instructors, as all students in the class would have been less than fully competent speakers of English. Second, we could have provided Ricardo with opportunities to meet native speakers of English (for one method, see Krashen, 1978e). These speakers may have provided him with "foreigner-talk". A third possibility would have been to set up some mechanism for Ricardo to come into contact with other ESL acquirers, through an ESL or pull-out class or through some other means. As long as such a foreign student peer group had different first languages, this would have provided Ricardo with "interlanguage" input, another simpler code.

But would any of these simple codes have helped Ricardo acquire English? This is, I believe, a question of immense theoretical and applied interest, as fundamental as any in our field. On the theoretical level, it asks how acquirers acquire, or what "intake" is. On the applied level, it asks what sorts of environments are best for second (or first) language acquisition, a continuation of the discussion of formal and informal environments, previously dealt with by Krashen and Seliger (1975), d'Anglejan (1978), Tucker (1977), Stern (1978), Palmer (1978), and Chapter 3 of this volume.

Before discussing possible approaches to answering this question, some brief definitions are in order. We will focus on three sorts of simple codes that second language acquirers are apt to come into contact with. "Teacher-talk" is the classroom language that accompanies exercises, the language of explanations in second language and in some foreign language classrooms, and the language of classroom management. During break, it becomes "foreigner-talk" (see below). "Interlanguage talk" is simply the speech of other second language acquirers, often that of the foreign student peer group. It is, of course, fairly well described in the literature, but not dealt with as input. "Foreigner-talk" may be of two kinds. The term has been used to describe native speakers' imitations of second language speech or, rather, their acquisition of aspects of this interlanguage. As documented by Hatch, Shapira, and Wagner-Gough (1978), this may happen after prolonged contact with second language speakers. It is an extremely interesting phenomenon, but not of direct concern here. The sort of foreigner-talk that is relevant to our discussion is the simplified input native speakers may give to less than fully competent speakers of their language in communicative situations. It may range from the sort of foreigner-talk described by Ferguson (1975), aimed at very low-level speakers and characterized by pidginization-type grammatical changes, to very mild alterations in speech.

Whether these codes help the acquirer or not is an empirical question, and it is the purpose of this paper to suggest two possible approaches to investigating this issue. Each approach has its weaknesses—nevertheless, combined and perhaps supplemented, they may eventually help us to answer this basic question.

First, one can approach the question directly and ask whether acquirers who have had access to such codes actually acquire faster, and whether those who have not had access to these codes have had a harder time with second language acquisition. Another approach is to determine, from analyses of simple codes, whether they are linguistically appropriate for language acquisition. Some space is devoted below toward beginning investigation in both of these approaches. This is followed by discussion of some practices and attitudes in current language pedagogy.

The Gross Approach

The gross approach, or the "Good Language Learner" approach, is similar to "known good validity". Case histories are examined in order to determine whether those acquirers who encountered any of the three sorts of simple codes described above had more success in second language acquisition, and whether those with less experience with these codes did worse. The standard literature provides surprisingly little information on this issue,[1] other than the Wagner-Gough and Hatch's case histories mentioned above. I will therefore describe one case history, not as definitive evidence for or against the efficacy of simple codes in second language acquisition, but as a sample, an illustrative example of how this sort of data, despite the inevitable confounds and difficulties inherent with self-report, might shed light on this question.

Our subject is S. K., currently a professor of linguistics at a well-known university in Southern California. S. K. has attempted to acquire four different second languages during adulthood, two Indo-European (French and German) and two Semitic (Hebrew and Amharic). We first analyze the two Indo-European languages with respect to the amount of simple input S. K. experienced and his relative success (see Table 1).

Table 1. *Interaction with simple codes for subject "S. K."*

Target language	Teacher-talk	Interlanguage-talk	Foreigner-talk
German	+	+	+
French	+	+	−
Hebrew	+	+	+
Amharic	−	−	+

(Details in text.)

S. K. reports that he received a relatively large amount of teacher-talk in both German and French. He attended a class in German as a second language during his entire 10-months stay in Vienna as a music student in his early 20's. The class was conducted entirely in German due to the presence of a linguistically heterogeneous student body. He also experienced a fair amount of teacher-talk in French, during a 1-month course in Paris at the Alliance Française, and more recently as a student in the Pucciani–Hamil method in French as a foreign language in Los Angeles. S. K. also informs us that interlanguage-talk was available to him in both French and German. During his first few months in Austria, he was a member of a "foreign-student peer group" composed of foreign students from many different countries. Since the only language these students had in common was German, it was the lingua franca of the group. S. K. reports that other foreign students were his closest friends during his first few months in Austria. In French, S. K. also reports that a similar peer group was formed during his 1 month in Paris, and that he also used French a good deal as a lingua franca, as a common language with nonnative speakers of French while a Peace Corps Volunteer in Ethiopia (see below) and as a temporary member of a kibbutz in Israel. S. K. reports differences, however, with respect to foreigner-talk. S. K. began meeting native speakers of German more frequently after a few months in Austria, native speakers who became friends, and who, S. K. reports, took into account his less than perfect control of German. By the time S. K. left Austria, he felt quite at home with German, and experienced no particular hardships in communicating and understanding in formal and informal situations. S. K. says he received very little of such foreigner-talk in French, having stayed in Paris only 1 month and never having had a circle of native French speakers as friends. Despite a similar amount of formal instruction in both French and German (about 3 years' study of each), S. K. reports that his German is much better. While he can express himself in French and easily read fairly difficult material, he reports serious problems in listening comprehension and less feel for phrasing and finding the right word.

To this point, this case history suggests that teacher-talk and interlanguage-talk may be useful for attaining low–intermediate levels of competence, and that foreigner-talk may provide a bridge to high intermediate and advanced levels of competence. This is supported by a consideration of S. K.'s experiences with Hebrew and Amharic.

S. K.'s Hebrew experiences took place on an "Ulpan" program over 5 months' time on a kibbutz in northern Israel. The class was taught entirely in Hebrew and lasted 4 hours per day. As in the cases above, S. K. also had a great deal of use of Hebrew as a common language with other foreigners, this time with other Ulpan class members. In addition, S. K. got to know many native Israelis on the kibbutz who modified their speech so that communication in Hebrew was possible. S. K.'s experiences with Amharic were quite different. The only formal instruction he received was as a Peace Corps trainee for 2 months in the United States. The language of the classroom was English, and the class focused on explanation of the Amharic writing system and rules of grammar. During his 2 years as a Peace Corps volunteer, S. K. never used Amharic as a lingua franca with other non-Ethiopians, as other common languages were used. In addition, despite his interest in the language, S. K. reported that few Ethiopians would speak to him in Amharic; S. K. was stationed near the capital, Addis Ababa, and used Amharic only with non-educated Ethiopians for instrumental purposes. Despite the fact that S. K. used Amharic daily for 2 years, he reports that his proficiency in that language is quite low. While he feels he has "acquired" Hebrew, and has some feel for correctness in that language, his Amharic feels artificial to him: he relies a great deal on English surface syntax with Amharic vocabulary, applying whatever grammar rules he remembers when he can, and understands only the simplest conversations.

The Amharic–Hebrew contrast is consistent with the hypothesis that simple codes like teacher-talk and interlanguage-talk are extremely useful in attaining initial levels of fluency, in acquiring (as opposed to learning). Again, this one case history is presented only as an example, and others are necessary to determine just how universal these experiences are.

Linguistic Analysis of Simple Codes

We turn now to a different approach, the linguistic analysis of simple codes. This analysis is done with one goal in mind: to determine whether the inputs provided by teacher-talk, interlanguage-talk, and foreigner-talk are linguistically appropriate, that is, whether they can serve as true "intake" for language acquisition. To do this, we will first examine caretaker speech, language addressed to young children acquiring their first language, and discuss how this simple code might encourage language acquisition on the part of the child. We will then compare our conclusions for caretaker speech with what is known of the simple codes we are dealing with here.

Caretaker Speech and Language Acquisition

A great deal of current literature confirms that the speech directed to children acquiring first languages is different from adult native speaker–native speaker speech. It is known to be composed of shorter sentences, it is more intelligible, contains utterances that are more well formed, with less subordination, has a more restricted vocabulary, and refers to a more restricted range of topics (i.e. the "here and now"), among other features. Of course, "the finding that mother-ese exists cannot by itself show that it influences language growth" (Newport, Gleitman, and Gleitman, 1977; p. 112). If caretaker speech does help, or "catalyze" language acquisition, it may do so by supplying crucial input, what the child needs at that moment, without the distraction of excess noise, or language the child does not understand. The following section expands on this point in more detail. I present first three "facts" about child language acquisition and caretaker speech, followed by a personal interpretation as to how and why caretaker speech might be effective. Following this, we explore the question of whether the simple codes the second language performer might encounter work the same way.

Here are the three "facts". First, it is by now a well-established finding that structures are acquired in a relatively predictable order for children acquiring a given language (for English, see Brown, 1973; Klima and Bellugi, 1966; and the excellent review in Clark and Clark, 1977). This is not to say that order of acquisition is absolutely invariant, that children will acquire all grammatical structures in a strict linear order; rather, there are clear tendencies and one can talk about an "average" order of acquisition.

Another finding relevant to our discussion deals with the relationship between the complexity of structure in parental input and the child's current linguistic level. While caretaker speech is typically simpler than native speaker–native speaker speech, it is not "finely tuned" to the child's growing competence. According to studies by Newport et al. (1977) and Cross (1977), the syntactic complexity of caretaker speech does not grow in exact proportion to the child's competence. Caretaker speech, however, may be "roughly tuned" to the child's level: we see positive, but not always significant, correlations between structural complexity of caretaker speech, and linguistic maturity in children. Some sample correlations are presented in Table 2.

Table 2. *Degree of fine-tuning in caretaker speech*

Input characteristics	Child language variables					
	VP aux.[a]	NP infl.[a]	MLU[a]	MLU[b]	compr.[b]	age[b]
S-node/utterance	0.21	−0.05	0.37	0.30	0.55*	0.36
MLU	0.34	0.10	0.37	0.56*	0.75†	0.51*

a: Newport, Gleitman, and Gleitman, 1977.
b: Cross, 1977.

Key:
VP aux. = auxiliaries such as modals, progressive and perfective elements.
NP infl. = nominal inflections, primarily plural markers.
MLU = mean length utterance.
compr. = score on a comprehension measure (see Cross, p. 157).
age = child's age in weeks.
$* = p < 0.05$.
$† = p < 0.01$.

The third "fact" of interest to us here is that according to scholars working in the area of child language acquisition, the relative "simplicity" of caretaker speech is probably not due to any conscious effort on the part of the caretaker to teach language. Rather, caretakers modify their speech in order to communicate with children, in order to control their behavior, in order to make them understand what they are saying. (For detailed discussion, see especially Newport *et al.*, pp. 124–130.)

These three findings lead to the following generalization concerning the relationship of input and the child's developing grammar. Children progress by *understanding* language that is a little beyond them. That is, if a child is at a stage i, that child can progress to stage $i + 1$ along the "natural sequence" (where i and $i + 1$ may be a block of structures; more correctly the child who has just acquired the members of i can then acquire a member of $i + 1$) by understanding language containing $i + 1$. The child understands language containing structure that is a bit beyond him or her with the aid of context. The fact that caretaker speech is so well rooted in the "here and now" probably provides this helpful context to a great extent. (It is of interest that the "here and now" quality of caretaker speech is one of its "best tuned" aspects: Cross (1977) reports strong correlations between the degree to which parental speech is concerned with immediate events and the child's competence: more linguistically mature children encounter more discourse that is displaced in time and space ($r = 0.72$, $p < 0.01$ between reference to "non-immediate events" and scores on a comprehension test).)

Caretaker speech does provide input at the $i+1$ level that is understood, but, as explained above, this is not the conscious goal of the caretaker. The caretaker is not consciously aiming at $i+1$. Rather, the caretaker estimates the child's level of competence via the child's own linguistic output and his or her reactions to caretaker speech, and in attempting to communicate with the child provides input that covers $i+1$ as well as some structures that the child has already acquired (i, $i-n$) and some that the child has not yet acquired ($i+n$). In other words, the caretaker's speech provides a "net" of structure that generally includes $i+1$, but contains a bit more. The size of the net, however, is not as large as is the case in adult–adult speech.

A very interesting hypothesis is that the net of structure cast by caretaker speech in an attempt to communicate with the child *is of optimal size*. A wider net might contain too much noise, too much language that is not understood by the child, for optimum acquisition. A more narrow net, a "finely-tuned" net hitting $i+1$ and little else, may also be less efficient. The caretaker's net may have these advantages: by dealing with some of the $i-n$ and $i+n$ structures, by dealing with more than $i+1$, it provides built-in anticipation and review, which may be useful. Second, the wider, roughly-tuned net guarantees that $i+1$ will always be covered. Also, a wider net allows more than one child to be helped at one time. On the other hand, the caretaker net is not so wide that the child has difficulty understanding, and "tunes out" (see, for example, Shipley, Smith, and Gleitman, 1969).

Brown (1977), after reviewing current studies of caretaker speech, suggests the following answer to the question "How can a concerned mother facilitate her child's learning of language?":

> Believe that your child can understand more than he or she can say, and seek, above all, to communicate. To understand and be understood. To keep your minds fixed on the same target. In doing that, you will, without thinking about it, make 100 or maybe 1000 alterations in your speech and action. Do not try to practice them as such. There is no set of rules of how to talk to a child that can even approach what you unconsciously know. If you concentrate on communicating, everything else will follow (p. 26).

These comments are clearly in the spirit of the above discussion.

The position outlined here maintains and refines some of my earlier hypotheses. In Chapter 8 it was claimed that speaking is *theoretically* unnecessary for acquisition, but may serve to encourage appropriate input (input with the proper size "net"). Acquisition (as opposed to learning), it was claimed, is the result of input, or intake, not actual production. Here, it is suggested that the adult uses the child's output as a part of the information he or she needs to estimate the child's current level of competence. Strictly speaking, however, speaking is not necessary.

We turn now to simple codes the second language acquirer might face, to see whether they might have an effect similar to that of caretaker speech on second language acquisition.

Simple Codes and Second Language Acquisition

All three simple codes discussed above, teacher-talk, interlanguage-talk, and foreigner-talk, are clearly attempts to communicate. The question we thus need to ask is whether the "net" they cast is the same size, and whether they might have the same effect as caretaker speech on language acquisition.

The "facts" about child language acquisition and caretaker speech seem to hold true for simple codes and second languages. In the first place, current research supports the hypothesis that structure emerges in second language performers in a more or less predictable order for adults (Bailey, Madden, and Krashen, 1974; Krashen, Sferlazza, Feldman, and Fathman, 1976; Fuller, 1978; Hyltenstam, 1977), revealed when testing is done in "Monitor-free" conditions (Chapter 4, this volume).

The available data indicate, moreover, that the simple codes we are concerned with are "tuned" to about the same degree as caretaker speech is: they are simpler than native speaker–native speaker speech, and are not "finely tuned" to the level of the acquirer, but one sees signs of "rough tuning". To illustrate this point, I present a brief survey of the literature available to me at this time, arranged according to input features:

1. *Rate*. There is evidence that caretaker speech is at least roughly tuned with respect to rate of speech. Broen (1972) compared rate of speech to 5- and 2-year-olds, and found that younger children received slower input. Also, Cross (1977) reports a 0.36 (ns) correlation between rate of input to fast acquirers and their age. On the other hand, Cross found no relation between rate of input speech and the children's linguistic competence, as measured by a test of comprehension ($r = -0.12$, ns).

For teacher-talk, Henzl (1973), investigating the behavior of Czech speakers, concluded that teacher-talk was slower than native speaker–native speaker speech, but did not look for signs of fine tuning. Trager (1978) confirmed Henzl's findings for ESL at USC, and found some signs of tuning, with beginning ESL students receiving slower input than intermediate and advanced students. A recent study by Brunak and Scarcella (1979) confirms that interlanguage-talk is slower than native speaker speech. Also, I know of no data on foreigner-talk.

2. *Lexicon*. Broen (1972) reports that younger children receive a lower type/token ratio, supporting at least rough tuning for age for caretaker speech. Henzl (1973) also found that teacher-talk had a lower type/token ratio than native speaker–native speaker speech but did not look for tuning. Trager (1978) again confirmed Henzl's results, but found no evidence for tuning by level in ESL. Again, I know of no data for interlanguage-talk, but it is probably simpler in lexicon. For foreigner-talk, Robertson (1978), in a small-scale study (two ESL acquirers and two native speakers), concluded that the less advanced ESL performer received a lower type/token ratio.

3. *Well formedness*. Caretaker speech, according to Newport *et al.* (1977), is "unswervingly well formed". Newport *et al.*, however, report that there is no evidence for tuning: caretaker speech is more well formed than adult–adult speech, but less mature children do not receive better formed input than more mature children. Cross (1977), however, reports good correlations for well formedness and linguistic

development ($r = 0.56$, $p < 0.05$). This difference may be due to sample differences; Cross' sample consisted of children known to be rapid acquirers.

Henzl (1973) reports that teacher-talk is better formed than native speaker–native speaker speech. This was confirmed by Wiley (1978), who also found some signs of tuning: her beginning ESL students heard fewer disfluencies than did intermediate and advanced students. Freed (1980) reported that in her study of Americans talking to ESL performers, foreigner-talk appeared to be about as well formed as caretaker speech (compared to Newport, 1976). There are no data for interlanguage-talk, which is probably not as well formed as native speaker–native speaker speech.

4. *Length*. Caretaker speech is shorter than adult–adult speech but, as Newport *et al.* point out, this does not necessarily mean simpler. As seen in Table 1, Cross (1977) finds evidence for at least rough tuning, but Newport *et al.* do not. As mentioned above, this may be due to sample differences. Henzl confirms that teacher-talk is shorter than native speaker–native speaker speech, but did not search for tuning. Again, there are no data for interlanguage-talk and foreigner-talk.

5. *Propositional complexity*. As seen in Table 1, there is some evidence for rough tuning in caretaker speech for this feature: there are generally positive correlations (but not usually significant) between the number of S nodes per utterance in the input and the child's linguistic maturity, again with higher correlations found in Cross' study. Trager (1978) used this measure for input to second language acquirers, finding again that teacher-talk is less complex than native speaker–native speaker talk, and also that beginners received somewhat less complex input than intermediate and advanced students.

Other scholars have used other measures. Both Gaies (1977) and Wiley (1978) used T-unit-based measures, such as words per T-unit and clauses per T-unit. Briefly, both studies agree that teacher-talk is simpler than native speaker–native speaker speech. Gaies, however, found evidence for tuning by level, his beginners receiving simpler input than his intermediates, and his intermediates receiving simpler input than his advanced ESL students. Wiley, with a slightly smaller sample, did not find evidence for tuning by level. Henzl also reports less subordination in teacher-talk.

Freed (1980) reports that foreigner-talk is "strikingly similar" to caretaker speech with respect to grammatical complexity, as measured by the average number of S nodes per utterance (compared to Newport, 1976). Moreover, Freed reports at least some signs of tuning: native English speakers talking to "low foreigners" produced utterances tending to have fewer S nodes per utterance as compared to English speakers talking to "high foreigners", while input to both groups was less complex than native speaker–native speaker speech.

It is probably safe to assume that interlanguage-talk is less complex than native speaker–native speaker speech with respect to propositional complexity.[2]

While the data are sparse, they are consistent with the hypothesis that these simple codes are roughly tuned to the level of the listener, possibly to the same degree as is caretaker speech. The size of the net might be about right, and it may be cast in the same way, by a communicator interested in getting his or her conversational partner to understand. For all three simple codes it may be the case that communication casts an optimal size net.

Before concluding that simple codes are optimal for language acquisition, we need to consider several problems. First, there are some differences between caretaker speech and the simple codes we are discussing. Caretaker speech typically contains high proportions of imperatives and questions, while teacher-talk (Trager, 1978) and foreigner-talk (Free, 1980) appear to contain a larger percentage of declaratives. Is this a crucial difference? Also, there is the obvious ungrammaticality of interlanguage talk. While caretaker speech also contains occasional examples of what might be considered ungrammatical forms (e.g. uninverted yes/no question), interlanguage input is probably even more ungrammatical. Do the virtues of this simple code outweigh any problems caused by these errors? Also, even if simple codes are useful, if the acquirer hears only these codes we can expect fossilization: teacher-talk may be inherently limited due to the limitation of what can be discussed in the classroom, while interlanguage-talk is of course limited by the competence of the speakers. As for foreigner-talk, not all foreign-talkers may be good "language teachers", not all native speakers will lay down the right size "net". (Mark Twain complained that even though he had learned "intermediate French", he found no one who spoke this dialect when he got to Paris.)

To summarize: if caretaker speech is helpful for language acquisition, it may be the case that simple codes are useful in much the same way. The teacher, the more advanced second language performer, and the native speaker in casual conversation, in attempting to communicate with the second language acquirer, may unconsciously make the "100 or maybe 1000 alterations in his speech" that provide the acquirer with optimal input for language acquisition.

Re-analysis of Classroom Exercises

In the previous sections, I have attempted to state the following hypothesis: simple codes such as teacher-talk, interlanguage-talk, and foreigner-talk aid second language acquisition for adults in much the same way that caretaker speech aids child language acquisition. If this is the case, if our hypothesis is supported by subsequent research, we can then ask how classroom exercises compare to simple codes. In this section, I anticipate this discussion with some general comments on the role of classroom exercises.

There are various possibilities for classroom exercises. First, they can be classified as to whether their focus is on gaining formal or conscious knowledge of the target language (Monitor), or whether their goal is on gaining acquired or subconscious knowledge. The former are grammar exercises, the latter communicative exercises. Of course, some exercises may do both at once, but we will find it useful to maintain this distinction for the moment.

Classroom exercises, in considering one grammatical structure of the target language at a time, may vary as to whether they "hit" the acquirer's $i + 1$ structure(s). An exercise may undershoot, hitting a structure that has already been acquired, it may overshoot, hitting far beyond $i + 1$, and of course it may hit the target, $i + 1$.

For drills that focus on *acquisition*, even if they manage to hit the target, $i + 1$, we may question whether they actually provide *enough* input for real acquisition to occur. Also, they typically lack the anticipation and review that simple codes provide automatically. When acquisition-type activities undershoot, the result of course may be boredom. When they overshoot, the result will be frustration.

For drills that focus on *learning*, undershooting may produce either boredom, or, occasionally, for interested amateur linguists in a class, "language appreciation" (see remarks in Chapter 8). If a learning exercise is "on target" or in advance of $i + 1$, the result will be a contribution to the conscious Monitor, if the exercise is successful. As discussed previously, Monitor use has its advantages, but also has its limits.

The use of simple codes may thus have some real advantages over classroom exercises. The latter take deliberate aim at the $i + 1$th structure; when they miss it, as is probable for some students in a large class, the results are of dubious value. Even when they hit it, there may be a need for more review and we can question whether the quantity of input was sufficient (witness the constant need for review in second and foreign language classes; for the latter, the second year is often exclusively devoted to a review of grammar presented the first year). Simple codes, however, provide a "shot-gun" approach that may cover the $i + 1$ with built-in review.

Finally, many classroom exercises, with their emphasis on correctness, often place the student "on the defensive" (Stevick, 1976), entailing a heightened "affective filter" (Dulay and Burt, 1977), which makes them less than ideal for language acquisition. The use of simple informal codes, on the other hand, generally occurs in situations where the focus is on communication and not form, and where the filter is "down" or at least much weaker. In Stevick's terms, this allows the input to strike more "deeply" and thus be more effective intake for acquisition. (For discussion, see Stevick, 1976; Chapter 2, this volume.)[3]

Some Final Comments: A Summer as an Intermediate French Student

By way of conclusion, I would like to report on some recent personal experiences as a student of French. The class I attended in the summer of 1978 in Los Angeles was a private class, with a small number of highly motivated, highly intelligent, and mature students. The official "method" used was the Pucciani–Hamel approach (Langue et Langage), used with much apparent success at UCLA and at many other schools. The method is "inductive", that is, students are led to induce, or guess, the rules. In a typical lesson, the teacher asks what are hopefully meaningful, interesting questions of members of the class in hopes of preparing a context for the target structure. The following exchange is a good example (taken from the instructor's manual, Pucciani and Hamel, 1974; p. 321). The purpose in this exercise is to teach the conjunction "bien que" and the fact that its presence requires that the following verb be in the subjunctive mood:

Teacher: Fait-il beau aujourd'hui?
Student: Non, il ne fait pas beau maintenant.
Teacher: Irez-vous cependant à la plage pendant le week-end?
Student: Oui, j'irai cependant à la plage pendant le week-end.
Teacher: Irez-vous à la plage bien qu'il ne fasse pas beau?
Student: Oui, j'irai à la plage bien qu'il ne . . .

My excellent teacher followed this sort of pattern, and often tailored questions to individual students' interests. For example, one member of the class was a dedicated beachgoer, and the example given above was actually used with this student. My teacher also allowed some "free-play". If the student did not give her the structure she was looking for, she tolerated some "conversation", as long as it was in French (a cornerstone of the Pucciani–Hamil approach is the exclusive use of the target language in the classroom). Indeed, despite the fact that the class was a first-year (third quarter) level class, it often had the flavor of a conversation class.

The explicit goal of the class was learning, conscious control of structure. There was error correction, and after enough examples of the above sort had been elicited, there was explanation of the rule (in French), along with further examples if necessary.

What is particularly interesting is that many of the students felt that the obvious success of this class was due to grammar work. One excellent student (a man in his sixties) felt he needed to "firm up" his grammar before doing conversation in French, and he told me that he felt our teacher's finest quality was her ability to explain complex rules of French grammar. My hypothesis is that much of the success of the class was due to the teacher's use of teacher-talk, her ability to provide a simple code that provided nearly optimal input for acquisition. The class was conducted entirely in French, as mentioned above. Besides the actual pedagogical examples, such as exchanges of the sort given above, teacher-talk included explanation of grammar and vocabulary, the teacher's participation in the "free play" surrounding the exercises, mentioned above, occasional anecdotes, classroom management, etc. My fellow students reported that they understood nearly everything the teacher said in class. The teacher-talk, not the grammar *per se*, was probably what motivated the same student who needed to firm up his grammar to comment: "She gives you a feeling for French . . . she makes you *want* to speak French." This is language acquisition, not language learning.

One example is worth mentioning. One session, the phrase "telle ou telle" came up in one of the readings. After several attempts to supply synonyms and explain by example what this expression meant, our teacher gave up. She had failed to make us understand what "telle ou telle" meant, and she felt bad, thinking she had wasted several minutes of valuable classtime. According to my interpretation, the time was not wasted at all. For five minutes, we had the benefit of excellent input; we were understanding and acquiring French.

This particular class may have been so successful because the members of the class were good Monitor users who were getting both acquisition and learning at the same time. Certainly, one can learn grammar in the mother tongue, and one can receive good input without instruction in grammar. If acquisition alone were the goal, the class could have been in nearly any subject-matter of interest. These students, however, were interested in the structure of French and believed that learning structure formally would help them. This belief and attitude focused them *off* form and on communication for the teacher-talk, and *on* form for their use of grammar in exercises. They were thus getting both learning and acquisition, from an approach that seems to be well suited to the good Monitor user interested in language (see also the description of the "traditional approach" used in the Canadian Public Service Commission Language Training Branch, described in Wesche, 1980).

Despite the fact that I am perfectly capable of studying French grammar on my own, the class was immensely valuable. In fact, if I were a second language acquirer in another country, I would happily go to class. The least of my goals would be to learn grammar. There is valuable teacher-talk to listen to (on a topic I happen to be interested in, grammar: I realize that I am a member of perhaps a small minority), other students to meet for interlanguage talk, and through the teacher and the other students, possible contacts with native speakers who might provide me with useful foreigner-talk.

The efficacy of simple codes in providing input for language acquisition is an empirical issue, one which I have undoubtedly oversimplified. But, paraphrasing John Oller, it will not be resolved by taking a vote, and is not a matter of opinion or taste. It can be tested using a variety of approaches, and there is enough suggestive evidence already to hypothesize that simple codes are of tremendous help to acquirers at early and intermediate stages, child and adult, first and second languages.

Notes

[1] The second language acquisition literature does contain some hints, although no one, to my knowledge, has explicitly addressed the question of whether simple codes help. Palmer (1979) compared control and experimental EFL classes in Thailand, where the control class received "traditional" instruction, including teacher-talk in English, and the experimental class used "language games", a peer communication activity designed by Palmer and Kimball (1978). The experimental group showed higher correlations between communicative and grammar-type tests, which might be considered a sign of language acquisition (Palmer, 1978). Nevertheless, despite the greater emphasis on communication in the experimental class, Palmer found no significant differences between the groups on communicative measures. This may be due, he suggests, to the fact that the control group received more teacher-talk in English. The experimental group had the games explained in the first language (Thai). Palmer notes that in the experimental classes, "in order to complete two games . . . per period, almost all informal communication in English was eliminated from the classroom" (p. 17). Another hint is found in the "Good Language Learner" study of Naimon, Fröhlich, Stern, and Todesco (1978). Their thirty-four "good language learners" reported a preference for second language classes in the immersion situation, rather than foreign language study at home. One essential difference between second language and foreign language classes is the presence of obligatory teacher-talk in the target language in the former. Another is the possibility of interlanguage talk. Finally, Fathman (1976) studied young ESL students in Washington, D.C. and reported that "the students in schools where there were more than 40 non-native English speakers seemed to make more progress than those in schools where there were fewer foreign students" (p. 437). We cannot, of course, simply conclude that this was due to the interlanguage talk they received, but this is a testable hypothesis for future studies.

[2] The caretaker speech literature also reports that less mature children hear significant-

ly more expansions as well as repetitions from caretakers (Cross, 1977). This may also be the case for teacher-talk (Gaies, 1977, affirms that this is the case, but presents no statistics). It is not, however, clear that this means that expansions and repetitions are useful for the acquirer, although they may be. Cross (1977), Newport *et al.* (1977), and R. Brown (1977) suggest that expansions are communication checks: less mature children hear more of them because the mother needs to check more.

Similarly, Cross (1977, p. 167) says that caretaker repetition comes from the child's failure to understand, and the need to repeat naturally decreases over time. This is not to say that repetition and expansion do not help, just that it is far from clear that they do. (See also Nelson, Carskaddon, and Bonvillian, 1973.)

[3] Another possible advantage of simple informal input over standard classroom practice is the possibility of exposure to different discourse types and to different pragmatic uses of language. As has been pointed out several times in recent years (Wilkins, 1976; Long, 1975, 1976), classroom use of language (and this may include teacher-talk) is severely limited in terms of language *use,* in terms of communicative functions. According to Wilkins, "language learning (in classrooms) has concentrated much more on the use of language to report and describe than on doing things through language" (Wilkins, p. 42). A major pedagogical goal in recent years has been to provide in-class activities that will provide practice in various communicative functions of language; e.g. Long (1975) discusses the possibility of group work, an in-class interlanguage-talk, as a partial solution to this problem. Also, the "notional syllabus" suggested by Wilkins has as its goal the utilization of the classroom for helping students learn or acquire rules of communication. The simplified informal environment, however, may provide a built-in notional syllabus, complete with review and sufficient repetition for successful acquisition of communicative competence. We need to determine how much communicative competence is successfully acquired or learned by second language performers who have had primarily simplified informal experience with the target language as compared to those who have had primarily classroom experience.

Bibliography

Alajouanine, T. (1956) "Verbal realization in aphasia." *Brain* 79: 95–133.

Andersen, R. (1976) "A functional acquisition hierarchy study in Puerto Rico." Paper presented at the 10th annual TESOL conference, New York, New York. March 1976.

Andersen, R. (1977) "The impoverished state of cross-sectional morpheme acquisition/accuracy methodology." Paper presented at Los Angeles Second Language Acquisition Research Forum, UCLA, February 1977.

Asher, J. (1965) "The strategy of the total physical response: an application to learning Russian." *International Journal of Applied Linguistics* 3: 291–300.

Asher, J. (1966) "The learning strategy of the total physical response: a review." *Modern Language Journal* 50: 79–84.

Asher, J. (1969) "The total physical response approach to second language learning." *Modern Language Journal* 53: 3–17.

Ausubel, D. and P. Ausubel (1971) "Cognitive development in adolescence." In H. Thornburg (Ed.), *Contemporary Adolescence: Readings.* Belmont, California: Brooks-Cole, pp. 42–49.

Bailey, N., C. Madden, and S. Krashen (1974) "Is there a 'natural sequence' in adult second language learning?" *Language Learning* 21: 235–243.

Banathy, B., E. Trager, and C. Waddle (1966) "The use of contrastive data in foreign language course development." In A. Valdman (Ed.), *Trends in Language Teaching.* New York: McGraw-Hill, pp. 35–56.

Barton, M., H. Goodglass, and A. Shai (1965) "Differential recognition of tachistoscopically presented English and Hebrew words in right and left visual fields." *Perceptual and Motor Skills* 21: 431–437.

Bialystok, E. and M. Fröhlich (1977) "Aspects of second language learning in classroom settings." *Working Papers on Bilingualism* 13: 1–26.

Birnbaum, R. (1976) "Transcription and analysis of the speech of an adult second language learner." Term Paper, Dept. of Linguistics, University of Southern California.

Birnbaum, R., J. Butler, and S. Krashen (1977) "The use of the Monitor in free and edited ESL compositions." Paper presented at the Los Angeles Second Language Acquisition Forum. UCLA, February, 1977.

Bogen, J. (1969a) "The other side of the brain. I: Dysgraphia and dyscopia following cerebral commissurotomy." *Bulletin of the Los Angeles Neurological Society* 34: 73–105.

Bogen, J. (1969b) "The other side of the brain. II: An appositional mind." *Bulletin of the Los Angeles Neurological Society* 34: 135–162.

Bogen, J. and G. Bogen (1969) "The other side of the brain. III: The corpus callosum and creativity." *Bulletin of the Los Angeles Neurological Society* 34: 191–200.

Brière, E. (1966) "Quality versus quantity in second language composition." *Language Learning* 16: 141–151.

Broen, P. (1972) *The Verbal Environment of the Language Learning Child.* ASHA Monograph number 17. Washington, D.C.: American Speech and Hearing Association.

Brown, H. D. (1977) "Cognitive and affective characteristics of good language learners." Paper presented at Los Angeles Second Language Acquisition Research Forum, UCLA, February 1977.

Brown, H. D., C. Yorio, and R. Crymes (1977) (Eds.) *On TESOL '77: Teaching and Learning English as a Second Language: Trends in Research and Practice.* Washington, D.C.: TESOL.

Brown, R. (1973) *A First Language.* Cambridge: Harvard Press.

Brown, R. (1977) "Introduction to Snow and Ferguson." In C. Snow and C. Ferguson (Eds.), *Talking to Children.* New York: Cambridge University Press, pp. 1–27.

Brown, R. and C. Hanlon (1970) "Derivational complexity and order of acquisition in child speech." In J. Hayes (Ed.), *Cognition and the Development of Language.* New York: Wiley, pp. 155–207.

Brown, R., C. Cazden, and U. Bellugi (1973) "The child's grammar from I to III." In C. Ferguson and D. Slobin (Eds.), *Studies of Child Language Development.* New York: Holt, Rinehart, and Winston, pp. 295–333.

Brunak, J. and R. Scarcella (1979) "On speaking politely in a second language," Paper presented at 13th Annual TESOL Conference, Boston, March 1979.

Burt, M., H. Dulay, and E. Hernandez (1975) *The Bilingual Syntax Measure.* New York: Harcourt, Brace, Jovanovich.

Buteau, M. (1970) "Students' errors in the learning of French as a second language." *International Review of Applied Linguistics* 7: 133–146.

Butterworth, G. (1972) "A Spanish-speaking adolescent's acquisition of English syntax." MA Thesis, UCLA TESL Department.

Caplan, P. and M. Kinsbourne (1976) "Baby drops the rattle: asymmetry of duration of grasp by infants." *Child Development* 47: 532–534.

Carmon, A. and I. Nachshon (1971) "Effects of unilateral brain damage on perception of temporal order." *Cortex* 7: 410–418.

Carroll, F. (1978) "The other side of the brain and foreign language learning." Paper presented at the 12th annual TESOL conference, Mexico City, April 1978.

Carroll, J. (1963) "The prediction of success in intensive foreign language training." In R. Glazer (Ed.), *Training Research and Education.* Pittsburgh: University of Pittsburgh Press.

Carroll, J. (1967) "Foreign language proficiency levels attained by language majors near graduation from college." *Foreign Language Annals* 1: 131–151.

Carroll, J. (1973) "Implications of aptitude test research and psycholinguistic theory for foreign language teaching." *Linguistics* 112: 5–13.

Carroll, J. (1977) "Characteristics of successful second language learners." In M. Burt, H. Dulay, and M. Finnochiaro (Eds.), *Viewpoints on English as a Second Language.* New York: Regents, pp. 1–7.

Cazden, C. (1968) "The acquisition of noun and verb inflections." *Child Development* 39: 433–448.

Cazden, C. (1972) *Child Language and Education.* New York: Holt, Rinehart, and Winston.

Cazden, C. (1975) "Hypercorrection in test responses: an example of test-induced distortions in children's speech." *Theory into Practice* 14: 343–345.

Chan, T. (1975) "Error analysis, contrastive analysis, and students' perception: a study of difficulty in second language learning." *International Review of Applied Linguistics* **13**: 119–143.

Chastain, K. (1975) "Affective and ability factors in second language learning." *Language Learning* **25**: 153–161.

Chihara, T. and J. Oller (1978) "Attitudes and attained proficiency in EFL: a sociolinguistic study of adult Japanese speakers." *Language Learning* **28**: 55–68.

Chomsky, N. (1964) *Current Issues in Linguistic Theory.* The Hague: Mouton.

Chomsky, N. (1965) *Aspects of the Theory of Syntax.* Cambridge: MIT Press.

Clark, H. and E. Clark (1977) *Psychology and Language.* New York: Harcourt, Brace, Jovanovich.

Clark, R. (1974) "Performing without competence." *Journal of Child Language* **1**: 1–10.

Cohen, A. and M. Robbins (1976) "Towards assessing interlanguage performance: the relationship between selected errors, learner's characteristics, and learner's explanations." *Language Learning* **26**: 45–66.

Corder, S. P. (1967) "The significance of learner's errors." *International Review of Applied Linguistics* **5**: 161–170.

Cross, T. (1977) "Mother's speech adjustments: the contribution of selected child listener variables," In C. Snow and C. Ferguson (Eds.), *Talking to Children.* New York: Cambridge University Press, pp. 151–188.

Curry, F. (1967) "A comparison of left-handed and right-handed subjects on verbal and non-verbal dichotic listening tasks." *Cortex* **3**: 343–352.

Curtiss, S. (1977) *Genie: A Psycholinguistic Study of a Modern Day "Wild Child".* New York: Academic Press.

Curtiss, S., V. Fromkin, and S. Krashen (1978) "Language development in the mature (minor) right hemisphere." *ITL: Review of Applied Linguistics* **39–40**: 23–37.

d'Anglejan, A. (1978) "Language learning in and out of classrooms." In J. Richards (Ed.), *Understanding Second and Foreign Language Learning.* Rowley, Ma.: Newbury House, pp. 218–236.

de Villiers, J. (1974) "Quantitative aspects of agrammaticism in aphasics." *Cortex* **10**: 36–54.

de Villiers, J. and P. de Villiers (1973) "A cross-sectional study of the acquisition of grammatical morphemes in child speech." *Journal of Psycholinguistic Research* **2**: 267–278.

Developmental Psychology Today (1971) New York: Ziff-Davis.

Diller, K. (1980) (Ed.) *Individual Differences and Universals in Language Learning Aptitude.* Rowley, Ma.: Newbury House.

Dore, J. (1974) "A developmental theory of speech act production." *Transactions of the New York Academy of Science.* New York.

Dulay, H. and M. Burt (1973) "Should we teach children syntax?" *Language Learning* **23**: 245–258.

Dulay, H. and M. Burt (1974a) "Natural sequences in child second language acquisition." *Language Learning* **24**: 37–53.

Dulay, H. and M. Burt (1974b) "Errors and strategies in child second language acquisition." *TESOL Quarterly* **8**: 129–136.

Dulay, H. and M. Burt (1975) "A new approach to discovering universal strategies of child second language acquisition." In D. Dato (Ed.), *Developmental Psycholinguistics: Theory and Applications.* Georgetown University Round Table on Languages and Linguistics. Washington: Georgetown University Press, pp. 209–233.

Dulay, H. and M. Burt (1977) "Remarks on creativity in language acquisition." In M. Burt, H. Dulay, and M. Finnochiaro (Eds.), *Viewpoints on English as a Second Language*. New York: Regents, pp. 95–126.

Duškova, L. (1969) "On sources of error in foreign language learning." *International Review of Applied Linguistics* 4: 11–36.

Elkind, D. (1970) *Children and Adolescents: Interpretive Essays on Jean Piaget*. New York: Oxford University Press.

Ervin, S. (1964) "Imitation and structural change in children's language." In E. Lenneberg (Ed.), *New Directions in the Study of Language*. Cambridge, Ma.: M.I.T. Press, pp. 163–189.

Ervin-Tripp, S. (1974) "Is second language learning like the first?" *TESOL Quarterly* 8: 111–127.

Fanselow, J. (1977) "The treatment of error in oral work." *Foreign Language Annals* 10: 583–593.

Fathman, A. (1975) "The relationship between age and second language productive ability." *Language Learning* 25: 245–266.

Fathman, A. (1976) "Variables affecting the successful learning of English as a second language," *TESOL Quarterly* 10: 433–441.

Felix, S. (1980) (Ed.) *Recent Trends in Research on Second Language Acquisition*. Tübingen: Gunter Narr.

Ferguson, C. (1971) *Statistical Analysis in Psychology and Education*. New York: McGraw-Hill.

Ferguson, C. (1975) "Toward a characterization of English foreigner talk." *Anthropological Linguistics* 17: 1–14.

Fillmore, L. (1976) *Cognitive and Social Strategies in Language Acquisition*. Ph.D. dissertation, Stanford University.

Freed, B. (1980) "Talking in children, talking to foreigners." In R. Scarcella and S. Krashen (Eds.), *Research in Second Language Acquisition*. Rowley, Ma.: Newbury House.

Friedlander, B., A. Jacobs, B. Davis, and H. Wetstone (1972) "Time-sampling analysis of infants' natural language environments in the home". *Child Development* 43: 730–740.

Fuller, J. Keyfetz (1978) *Natural and Monitored Sequences by Adult Learners of English as a Second Language*. Ph.D. dissertation, Florida State University.

Gaies, S. (1977) "The nature of linguistic input in formal language learning: linguistic and communicative strategies in ESL teachers' classroom language." In H. D. Brown, C. Yorio, and R. Crymes (Eds.), *Teaching and Learning English as a Second Language: Trends in Research and Practice. On TESOL '77*. Washington: TESOL, pp. 204–212.

Galloway, L. *The Cerebral Organization of Language in Bilinguals and Second Language Learners*. Ph.D. dissertation, UCLA (forthcoming).

Galloway, L. and R. Scarcella (1979) "Cerebral organization in adult second language acquisition." Presented at Linguistic Society of America, Los Angeles, December 1979.

Gardiner, M. and D. Walter (1976) "Evidence of hemispheric specialization from infant EEG." In S. Harnad, R. Doty, L. Goldstein, J. Jaynes, and G. Krauthamer (Eds.), *Lateralization in the Nervous System*. New York: Academic Press, pp. 481–502.

Gardner, R. (1960) "Motivational variables in second language learning." In R.

Gardner and W. Lambert, *Attitudes and Motivation in Second-Language Learning.* Rowley, Ma.: Newbury House.

Gardner, R. and W. Lambert (1959) "Motivational variables in second language acquisition." *Canadian Journal of Psychology* 13: 266–272.

Gardner, R. and W. Lambert (1965) "Language aptitude, intelligence, and second-language achievement." *Journal of Education Psychology* 56: 191–199. Reprinted in Gardner and Lambert (1972).

Gardner, R. and W. Lambert (1972) *Attitudes and Motivation in Second-Language Learning.* Rowley, Ma.: Newbury House.

Gardner, R., P. Smythe, R. Clement, and L. Gliksman (1976) "Second-language learning: a social-psychological perspective." *Canadian Modern Language Review* 32: 198–213.

Gary, J. Olmstead (1974) *The Effects on Children of Delayed Oral Practice in Initial Stages of Second Language Learning.* Ph.D. dissertation, UCLA.

Gary, J. Olmstead (1975) "Delayed oral practice in initial stages of second language learning." In M. Burt and H. Dulay (Eds.), *On TESOL '75: New Directions in Second Language Learning, Teaching, and Bilingual Education.* Washington: TESOL, pp. 89–95.

Gaziel, T., L. Obler, S. Benton, and M. Albert (1977) "The dynamics of lateralization in second language learning: sex and proficiency effects." Paper presented at Boston University Conference on Language Development, Boston, 1977.

Geschwind, N. and W. Levitsky (1968) "Human brain: left–right asymmetries in temporal speech region." *Science* 161: 186–187.

Gillis, M. and R. Weber (1976) "The emergence of sentence modalities in the English of Japanese-speaking children." *Language Learning* 26: 77–94.

Gingras, R. (1978) (Ed.) *Second Language Acquisition and Foreign Language Teaching.* Washington, D.C.: Center for Applied Linguistics.

Gordon, H. (1970) "Hemispheric asymmetries in the perception of musical chords." *Cortex* 6: 387–398.

Grauberg, W. (1971) "An error analysis in German of first-year university students." In G. Perren and J. Trim (Eds.), *Applications of Linguistics.* Cambridge, England: University Press, pp. 257–263.

Guiora, A., H. Lane, and L. Bosworth (1967) "An explanation of some personality variables in authentic pronunciation of a second language." In H. Lane and E. Zale (Eds.), *Studies in Language and Language Behavior.* New York: Appleton–Century–Crofts, pp. 261–266.

Guiora, A., B. Beit-Hallahmi, R. Brannon, C. Dull, and T. Scovel (1972) "The effects of experimentally induced changes into ego states on pronunciation ability in a second language: an exploratory study." *Comprehensive Psychiatry* 13: 421–428.

Guiora, A., R. Brannon, and C. Dull (1972) "Empathy and second language learning." *Language Learning* 22: 111–130.

Guiora, A., M. Paluszny, B. Beit-Hallahmi, J. Catford, R. Cooley, and C. Dull (1975) "Language and person: studies in language behavior." *Language Learning* 25: 43–61.

Hakuta, K. (1974) "A preliminary report on the development of grammatical morphemes in a Japanese girl learning English as a second language." *Working Papers on Bilingualism* 3: 18–43.

Hakuta, K. (1976) "A case study of a Japanese child learning English as a second language." *Language Learning* 26: 321–351.

Hakuta, K. and H. Cancino (1977) "Trends in second language acquisition research." *Harvard Educational Review* 47: 294–316.

Hale, T. and E. Budar (1970) "Are TESOL classes the only answer?" *Modern Language Journal* 54: 487–492.

Hamers, J. and W. Lambert (1977) "Visual field and cerebral hemisphere preferences in bilinguals." In S. Segalowitz and F. Gruber (Eds.), *Language Development and Neurological Theory*. New York: Academic Press, pp. 57–62.

Hanania, E. and H. Gradman (1977) "Acquisition of English structures: a case study of an adult native speaker in an English-speaking environment." *Language Learning* 27: 75–92.

Hatch, E. (1972) "Some studies in language learning". *UCLA Workpapers in Teaching English as a Second Language* 6: 29–36.

Hatch, E. (1976) "The metalinguistic awareness of child second language learners." Paper presented at USC-UCLA Second Language Acquisition Forum.

Hatch, E. (1978) "Discourse analysis and second language acquisition." In E. Hatch (Ed.), *Second Language Acquisition*. Rowley, Ma.: Newbury House, pp. 401–435.

Hatch, E., R. Shapira, and J. Wagner-Gough (1978) "'Foreigner-talk' discourse." *ITL: Review of Applied Linguistics* 39–40: 39–60.

Hécean, H. (1976) "Acquired aphasia in children and the ontogenesis of hemispheric functional specialization." *Brain and Language* 3: 114–134.

Henzl, V. (1973) "Linguistic register of foreign language instruction." *Language Learning* 23: 207–222.

Heyde, A. (1977) "The relationship between self-esteem and the oral production of a second language." In H. D. Brown, C. Yorio, and R. Crymes (Eds.), *On TESOL '77: Teaching and Learning English as a Second Language: Trends in Research and Practice*. Washington: TESOL, pp. 226–240.

Holdich, D. (1976) Unpublished term paper, UCLA, TESL Department.

Houck, N., J. Robertson, and S. Krashen (1978) "On the domain of the conscious grammar: morpheme orders for corrected and uncorrected ESL student transcriptions." *TESOL Quarterly* 12: 335–339.

Huang, J. (1971) *A Chinese Child's Acquisition of English Syntax*. MA Thesis, UCLA, TESL Department.

Huang, J. and Hatch, E. (1978) "A Chinese child's acquisition of English." In Hatch, E. (Ed.), *Second Language Acquisition*. Rowley, Ma.: Newbury House, pp. 118–131.

Hyltenstam, K. (1977) "Implicational patterns in interlanguage syntax variation." *Language Learning* 27: 383–411.

Inhelder, B. and J. Piaget (1958) *The Growth of Logical Thinking from Childhood to Adolescence*. New York: Basic Books.

Kellerman, E. (1978) "Giving learners a break: native language intuitions as a source of predictions about transferability." *Working Papers on Bilingualism* 15: 59–92.

Kellerman, E. (forthcoming) "Towards a characterisation of the strategy of transfer in second language learning".

Kershner, J. and A. Jeng (1972) "Dual functional hemispheric asymmetry in visual perception: effects of ocular dominance and post-exposural processes." *Neuropsychologia* 10: 437–445.

Kessler, C. (1975) "Postsemantic processes in delayed child language related to first and second language learning." In D. Dato (Ed.), *Developmental Psycholinguistics: Theory and Applications*. Georgetown University Round Table on Languages and Linguistics. Washington: Georgetown University, pp. 159–168.

Kessler, C. and I. Idar (1977) "The acquisition of English syntactic structures by a Vietnamese child." Paper presented at the Los Angeles Second Language Acquisition Forum, UCLA, 1977.

Kimura, D. (1961) "Cerebral dominance and the perception of verbal stimuli." *Canadian Journal of Psychology* 15: 166–171.

Klima, E. and U. Bellugi (1966) "Syntactic regularities in the speech of children." In J. Lyons and R. Wales (Eds.), *Psycholinguistic Papers*, Edinburgh: Edinburgh University Press, pp. 183–208.

Kounin, T. and S. Krashen (1978) "Approaching native speaker competence from two different directions." In C. Blatchford and J. Schachter (Eds.), *On TESOL '78: EFL Policies, Programs, Practices.* Washington: TESOL, pp. 205–212.

Krashen, S. (1973a) "Lateralization, language learning, and the critical period." *Language Learning* 23: 63–74.

Krashen, S. (1973b) "Mental abilities underlying linguistic and non-linguistic functions." *Linguistics* 115: 39–55.

Krashen, S. (1975a) "A model of second language performance." Paper presented at the winter meeting of the Linguistic Society of America, San Francisco, 1975.

Krashen, S. (1975b) "The critical period for language acquisition and its possible bases." In D. Aaronson and R. Rieber (Eds.), *Developmental Psycholinguistics and Communicative Disorders.* New York: New York Academy of Science, pp. 211–224.

Krashen, S. (1975c) "The development of cerebral dominance and language learning: More new evidence." In D. Dato (Ed.), *Developmental Psycholinguistics: Theory and Applications.* Georgetown University Round Table on Languages and Linguistics. Washington: Georgetown University, pp. 209–233.

Krashen, S. (1976a) "Formal and informal linguistic environments in language learning and language acquisition." *TESOL Quarterly* 10: 157–168.

Krashen, S. (1976b) "Cerebral asymmetry." In H. Whitaker and A. Whitaker (Eds.), *Studies in Neurolinguistics*, volume two. New York: Academic Press, pp. 157–191.

Krashen, S. (1977a) "Some issues relating to the Monitor Model." In H. D. Brown, C. Yorio, and R. Crymes (Eds.), *On TESOL '77: Teaching and Learning English as a Second Language: Trends in Research and Practice.* Washington: TESOL, pp. 144–158.

Krashen, S. (1977b) "The Monitor Model for adult second language performance." In M. Burt, H. Dulay, and M. Finocchiaro (Eds.), *Viewpoints on English as a Second Language.* New York: Regents, pp. 152–161.

Krashen, S. (1978a) "Individual variation in the use of the Monitor." In W. Ritchie (Ed.), *Principles of Second Language Learning.* New York: Academic Press, pp. 175–183.

Krashen, S. (1978b) "Adult second language acquisition and learning: a review of theory and practice." In R. Gingras (Ed.), *Second Language Acquisition and Foreign Language Teaching.* Washington, D.C.: Center for Applied Linguistics.

Krashen, S. (1978ċ) "Is the 'natural order' an artifact of the Bilingual Syntax Measure?" *Language Learning* 28: 175–183.

Krashen, S. (1978d) "Relating theory and practice in adult second language acquisition." *SPEAQ Journal* 2: 9–32.

Krashen, S. (1978e) "Language learning buttons." *Working Papers on Bilingualism* 15: 93–94.

Krashen, S. (1980a) "Attitude and aptitude in relation to second language acquisition and learning." In K. Diller (Ed.), *Individual Differences and Universals in Language*

Learning Aptitude. Rowley, Ma.: Newbury House.

Krashen, S. (1980b) "The theoretical and practical relevance of simple codes in second language acquisition." In R. Scarcella and S. Krashen (Eds.), *Research in Second Language Acquisition.* Rowley, Ma.: Newbury House.

Krashen, S., H. Seliger, and D. Hartnett (1974) "Two studies in adult second language learning." *Kritikon Litterarum* 2/3: 220–228.

Krashen, S. and P. Pon (1975) "An error analysis of an advanced ESL learner: the importance of the Monitor." *Working Papers on Bilingualism* 7: 125–129.

Krashen, S. and H. Seliger (1975) "The essential contributions of formal instruction in adult second language learning." *TESOL Quarterly* 9: 173–183.

Krashen, S. and H. Seliger (1976) "The role of formal and informal linguistic environments in adult second language learning." *International Journal of Psycholinguistics* 3: 15–21.

Krashen, S., V. Sferlazza, L. Feldman, and A. Fathman (1976) "Adult performance on the SLOPE test: more evidence for a natural order in adult second language acquisition." *Language Learning* 26: 145–151.

Krashen, S., N. Houck, P. Giunchi, S. Bode, R. Birnbaum, and G. Strei (1977) "Difficulty order for grammatical morphemes for adult second language performers using free speech." *TESOL Quarterly* 11: 338–341.

Krashen, S., J. Robertson, T. Loop, and K. Rietmann (1977) "The basis for grammaticality judgments in adult second language performance." Paper presented at Los Angeles Second Language Acquisition Research Forum, UCLA, 1977.

Krashen, S., J. Butler, R. Birnbaum, and J. Robertson (1978) "Two studies in language acquisition and language learning." *ITL: Review of Applied Linguistics* 39–40: 73–92.

Krashen, S. and L. Galloway (1978) "The neurological correlates of language acquisition." *SPEAQ Journal* 2: 21–35.

Krashen, S. and R. Scarcella (1978) "On routines and patterns in language acquisition and performance." *Language Learning* 28: 283–200.

Krashen, S., S. Zelinski, C. Jones, C. Usprich (1978) "How important is instruction?" *English Language Teaching Journal* 32: 257–261.

Lado, R. (1957) *Linguistics Across Cultures.* Ann Arbor, Mich.: University of Michigan Press.

Larsen-Freeman, D. (1975) "The acquisition of grammatical morphemes by adult ESL students." *TESOL Quarterly* 9: 409–420.

Lawler, J. and L. Selinker (1971) "On paradoxes, rules, and research in second language learning." *Language Learning* 21: 27–43.

Lee, R., L. McCune, and L. Patton (1970) "Physiological responses to different modes of feedback in pronunciation testing." *TESOL Quarterly* 4: 117–122.

Lenneberg, E. (1962) "Understanding language without ability to speak: a case report." *Journal of Abnormal and Social Psychology* 65: 419–425.

Lenneberg, E. (1967) *Biological Foundations of Language.* New York: Wiley.

LoCoco, V. (1975) "An analysis of Spanish and German learner's errors." *Working Papers on Bilingualism* 7: 96–124.

Long, M. (1975) "Group work and communicative competence in the ESOL classroom." In M. Burt and H. Dulay (Eds.), *New Directions in Second Language Learning, Teaching, and Bilingual Education.* Washington: TESOL, pp. 217–223.

Long, M. (1976) "Encouraging language acquisition by adults in a formal instructional setting." *ELT Documents* 76/3: 14–24.

Long, M. (1977) "Teacher feedback on learner error: mapping cognitions." In H. D. Brown, C. Yorio, and R. Crymes (Eds.), *On TESOL '77: Teaching and Learning English as a Second Language: Trends in Research and Practice*. Washington: TESOL, pp. 278–294.

Lukmani, Y. (1972) "Motivation to learn and language proficiency." *Language Learning* 22: 261–273.

Lyons, J. (1969) *Introduction to Theoretical Linguistics*. Cambridge: University Press.

Mason, C. (1971) "The relevance of intensive training in English as a foreign language for university students." *Language Learning* 21: 197–204.

Milner, B. (1962) "Laterality effects in audition." In V. Mountcastle (Ed.), *Interhemispheric Relations and Cerebral Dominance*. Baltimore: Johns Hopkins University Press, pp. 177–195.

Milon, J. (1974) "The development of negation in English by a second language learner." *TESOL Quarterly* 8: 137–143.

Molfese, D. (1976) "The ontogeny of cerebral asymmetry in man: auditory evoked potentials to linguistic and non-linguistic stimuli." In J. Desmedt (Ed.), *Recent Developments in the Psychology of Language: The Cerebral Evoked Potential Approach*. London: Oxford University Press.

Morgan, A., P. McDonald, and H. MacDonald (1971) "Differences in bilateral alpha activity as a function of experimental task, with a note on lateral eye movements and hypnotizability." *Neuropscyhologia* 9: 459–469.

Naimon, N., M. Fröhlich, D. Stern, and A. Todesco (1978) *The Good Language Learner*. Toronto: Ontario Institute for Studies in Education.

Nelson, K. (1975) "Individual differences in early semantic and syntactic development." In D. Aaronson and R. Rieber (Eds.), *Developmental Psycholinguistics and Communication Disorders*. New York: New York Academy of Science, pp. 132–139.

Nelson, K., G. Carskaddon, and J. Bonvillian (1973) "Syntax acquisition: impact of experimental variation in adult verbal interaction with the child." *Child Development* 44: 497–504.

Newmark, L. (1966) "How not to interfere with language learning." *Language Learning: The Individual and the Process. International Journal of American Linguistics* 40: 77–83.

Newmark, L. (1971) "A minimal language teaching program." In P. Pimsleur and T. Quinn (Eds.), *The Psychology of Second Language Learning*. Cambridge: University Press.

Newport, E. (1976) "Motherese: the speech of mothers to young children." In N. Castillan, D. Pisoni, and G. Potts (Eds.), *Cognitive Theory* vol. II. Hillsdale, New Jersey: Lawrence Eribaum Associates.

Newport, E., H. Gleitman, and L. Gleitman (1977) "Mother, I'd rather do it myself: some effects and non-effects of maternal speech style." In C. Snow and C. Ferguson (Eds.), *Talking to Children*. Cambridge: University Press, pp. 109–149.

Nida, E. (1956) "Motivation in second-language learning." *Language Learning* 7: 11–16.

Obler, L. (1980) "Right hemisphere participation in second language acquisition." In K. Diller (Ed.), *Individual Differences and Universals in Language Learning Aptitude*. Rowley, Ma.: Newbury House.

Obler, L., M. Albert, and H. Gordon (1975) "Asymmetry of cerebral dominance in Hebrew–English bilinguals." Paper presented at the 15th annual meeting of the

Academy of Aphasia. Victoria, British Columbia.

Oller, J. (1976a) "A program for language testing research." *Language Learning*, Special Issue no. 4, pp. 141–165.

Oller, J. (1976b) "'Evidence for a general language proficiency factor." *Die Neuren Sprachen* **2**: 165–174.

Oller, J. (1977) "Attitude variables in second language learning." In M. Burt, H. Dulay, and M. Finocchiaro (Eds.), *Viewpoints on English as a Second Language*. New York: Regents, pp. 172–184.

Oller, J. and F. Hinofotis (1976) "Two mutually exclusive hypotheses about second language proficiency: factor analytic studies of a variety of language tests." Paper presented at the winter meeting of the Linguistic Society of America, Philadelphia, December 1976.

Oller, J., L. Baca, and A. Vigil (1977) "Attitudes and attained proficiency in ESL: a sociolinguistic study of Mexican-Americans in the southwest." *TESOL Quarterly* **11**: 173–183.

Oller, J., A. Hudson, and P. Liu (1977) "Attitudes and attained proficiency in ESL: a sociolinguistic study of native speakers of Chinese in the United States." *Language Learning* **27**: 1–27.

Palmer, A. (1978) "Measures of achievement, communication, incorporation, and integration for two classes of formal ESL learners." Paper read at the 5th International Congress of Applied Linguistics, August 1978, Montreal, Canada.

Palmer, A. (1979) "Compartmentalized and integrated control: an assessment of some evidence for two kinds of competence and implications for the classroom." *Language Learning* **29**: 169–180.

Palmer, A. and M. Kimball (1978) "'Proper intake: a neglected component of formal instruction." *TESL Talk* **9**: 42–53.

Papcun, G., S. Krashen, D. Terbeek, R. Remington, and R. Harshman (1974) "The left hemisphere is specialized for speech, language, and/or something else." *Journal of the Acoustical Society of America* **55**: 319–327.

Peters, A. (1977) "Language learning strategies: does the whole equal the sum of its parts?" *Language* **53**: 560–573.

Pimsleur, P. (1966) "Testing foreign language learning." In A. Valdman (Ed.), *Trends in Language Teaching*. New York: McGraw-Hill, pp. 175–214.

Pimsleur, P., L. Mosberg, and A. Morrison (1962) "Student factors in foreign language teaching." *Modern Language Journal* **46**: 160–170.

Plann, S. and A. Ramirez (1976) "A study of the English and Spanish of Spanish speaking pupils in a Spanish immersion school program." *UCLA Working Papers in TESL, 1976*: 89–108.

Politzer, R. (1968) "An experiment in the presentation of parallel and contrasting structures." *Language Learning* **18**: 35–53.

Porter, R. (1977) "A cross-sectional study of morpheme acquisition in first language learners." *Language Learning* **27**: 47–62.

Postovsky, V. (1977) "Why not start speaking later?" In M. Burt, H. Dulay, and M. Finocchiaro (Eds.), *Viewpoints on English as a Second Language*. New York: Regents, pp. 17–26.

Pucciani, O. and J. Hamel (1974) *Langue et Langage*. New York: Holt, Rinehart, and Winston, 2nd edition.

Ravem, R. (1968) "Language acquisition in a second language environment." *IRAL* **6**: 175–185.

Richards, J. (1971) "Error analysis and second language strategies." *English Language Teaching* 25: 115–135.

Richards, J. (1975) "The context for error analysis." In M. Burt and H. Dulay (Eds.), *New Directions in Second Language Learning, Teaching and Bilingual Education. On TESOL '75.* Washington: TESOL, pp. 70–78.

Ritchie, W. (1978) (Ed.) *Principles of Second Language Learning.* New York: Academic Press.

Rivers, W. (1972) *Speaking in Many Tongues.* Rowley, Ma.: Newbury House.

Roberts, L. (1958) "Functional plasticity in cortical speech areas and the integration of speech." *Arch. Neurol. Psychiat. Chicago* 79: 275–283.

Robertson, J. (1978) "Variations in foreigner talk." Term paper, Dept. of Linguistics, USC.

Rogers, L., W. TenHouten, C. Kaplan, and M. Gardiner (1977) "Hemispheric specialization of language: an EEG study of bilingual Hopi Indian children." *International Journal of Neuroscience* 8: 1–6.

Rosansky, E. (1976) "Methods and morphemes in second language acquisition." *Language Learning* 26: 409–425.

Russell, R. and M. Espir (1961) *Traumatic Aphasia.* New York: Oxford University Press.

Satz, P., D. Bakker, J. Teunissen, R. Goebel, and H. Van der Vlugt (1975) "Developmental parameters of the ear asymmetry: a multivariate approach." *Brain and Language* 2: 171–185.

Savignon, S. (1976) "On the other side of the desk: a look at teacher attitude and motivation in second language learning." *Canadian Modern Language Review* 32: 295–302.

Scarcella, R. and S. Krashen (1980) (Eds.) *Research in Second Language Acquisition.* Rowley, Ma.: Newbury House.

Schumann, F. and J. Schumann (1977) "Diary of a language learner: an introspective study of second language learning." In H. D. Brown, C. Yorio, and R. Crymes (Eds.), *On TESOL '77: Teaching and Learning English as a Second Language: Trends in Research and Practice.* Washington: TESOL, pp. 241–249.

Schumann, J. (1975) "Affective factors and the problem of age in second language acquisition." *Language Learning* 25: 209–235.

Scovel, T. (1969) "Foreign accents, language acquisition and cerebral dominance." *Language Learning* 19: 245–254.

Seliger, H. (1977) "Does practice make perfect? A study of interaction patterns and L2 competence." *Language Learning* 27: 263–278.

Seliger, H., S. Krashen, and P. Ladefoged (1975) "Maturational constraints in the acquisition of a native-like accent in second language learning." *Language Sciences* 36: 20–22.

Selinker, L. (1972) "Interlanguage." *International Review of Applied Linguistics* 10: 209–231.

Selinker, L., M. Swain, and G. Dumas (1975) "The interlanguage hypothesis extended to children." *Language Learning* 25: 139–155.

Serafatinides, E. and M. Falconer (1963) "Speech disturbances in temporal lobe seizures: a study of 100 epileptic patients submitted to anterior temporal lobectomy." *Brain* 86: 333–346.

Shipley, E., C. Smith, and L. Gleitman (1969) "A study in the acquisition of language: free responses to commands." *Language* 45: 322–342.

Smith, A. (1966) "Speech and other functions after left (dominant) hemispherectomy." *Journal of Neurology, Neurosurgery, and Psychiatry* 29: 467–471.

Snow, C. and C. Ferguson (1977) (Eds.) *Talking to Children: Language Input and Acquisition.* Cambridge: Cambridge University Press.

Snow, C. and M. Hoefnagel-Hohle (1978) "Age differences in second language acquisition." In E. Hatch (Ed.), *Second Language Acquisition.* Rowley, Ma.: Newbury House, pp. 333–344.

Sorenson, A. (1967) "Multilingualism in the Northwest Amazon." *American Anthropologist* 69: 670–684.

Spolsky, B. (1969) "Attitudinal aspects of second language learning." *Language Learning* 19: 271–283.

Stafford, C. and G. Covitt (1978) "Monitor use in adult second language production." *ITL: Review of Applied Linguistics* 39–40: 103–125.

Stern, H. H. (1978) "The formal-functional distinction in language pedagogy: a conceptual clarification." Paper presented at the 5th International Congress of Applied Linguistics, August 1978, Montreal, Canada.

Stevick, E. (1976) *Memory, Meaning, and Method.* Rowley, Ma.: Newbury House.

Strei, G. (1976) "Acquisition data project." Term Paper, Department of Linguistics, University of Southern California.

Swain, M. and B. Burnaby (1976) "Personality characteristics and second language learning in young children: a pilot study." *Working Papers on Bilingualism* 11: 115–128.

Taylor, B. (1975) "The use of overgeneralization and transfer learning strategies by elementary and intermediate students in ESL." *Language Learning* 25: 73–107.

Taylor, L., A. Guiora, J. Catford, and H. Lane (1970) "Psychological variables and ability to pronounce a second language." *Language and Speech* 14: 146–157.

Terrell, T. (1977) "A natural approach to second language acquisition and learning." *Modern Language Journal* LXI: 325–337.

TESOL Quarterly 10, No. 2, June 1976, pp. 157–168.

Trager, S. (1978) "The language of teaching: discourse analysis in beginning, intermediate, and advanced ESL classrooms." MA paper, Department of Linguistics, USC.

Tucker, G. R. (1977) "Can a second language be taught?" In H. D. Brown, C. Yorio, and R. Crymes (Eds.), *On TESOL '77: Teaching and Learning English as a Second Language: Trends in Research and Practice.* Washington: TESOL, pp. 14–30.

Tucker, G. R., E. Hamayan, and F. Genesee (1976) "Affective, cognitive and social factors in second language acquisition." *Canadian Modern Language Review* 23: 214–226.

Turner, D. (1978) "The effect of instruction on second language learning and second language acquisition." Paper presented at 12th Annual TESOL Conference, Mexico City, April 1978.

Upshur, J. (1968) "Four experiments on the relation between foreign language teaching and learning." *Language Learning* 18: 111–124.

Van Lancker, D. (1972) *Heterogeneity in Language and Speech.* Ph.D. dissertation, UCLA Department of Linguistics. *UCLA Working Papers in Phonetics* 29.

von Elek, T. and M. Oskarsson (1973) *Teaching Foreign Language Grammar to Adults.* Stockholm: Almquist and Wiksell.

Wada, J., R. Clarke, and A. Hamm (1975) "Cerebral hemispheric asymmetry in humans." *Archives of Neurology* 32: 239–246.

Wagner-Gough, J. (1975) *Comparative Studies in Second Language Learning.* MA Thesis, UCLA, TESL Department.

Wagner-Gough, J. and E. Hatch (1975) "The importance of input data in second language acquisition studies." *Language Learning* 25: 297–308.

Wesche, M. (1977) "Learning behaviors of successful adult students on intensive language training." Paper presented at Los Angeles Second Language Acquisition Forum, UCLA, 1977.

Wesche, M. (1980) "Language aptitude measures in streaming, matching students with methodologies and diagnosis of learning problems." In K. Diller (Ed.), *Individual Differences and Universals in Language Learning Aptitude.* Rowley, Ma.: Newbury House.

Whitaker, H. (1971) *On the Representation of Language in the Human Mind.* Edmonton: Linguistic Research Inc.

Wiley, R. (1978) "An investigation of foreigner talk register in and out of the classroom." MA Paper, Dept of Linguistics, USC.

Wilkins, D. A. (1976) *Notional Syllabuses.* London: Oxford University Press.

Witelson, S. (1977) "Early hemisphere specialization and interhemispheric plasticity." In S. Segalowitz and F. Gruber (Eds.), *Language Development and Neurological Theory.* New York: Academic Press, pp. 213–287.

Witelson, S. and W. Pallie (1973) "Left hemisphere specialization for language in the newborn." *Brain* 96: 641–646.

Wode, H. (1978) "Developmental sequences in naturalistic L2 acquisition." In E. Hatch (Ed.), *Second Language Acquisition.* Rowley, Ma.: Newbury House, pp. 101–117.

Wode, H. (1979) "The L2 acquisition of English in a natural setting." *Studia Anglica Posnaniensia* 10: 35–48.

Wode, H., J. Bahns, H. Bedey, and W. Frank (1978) "Developmental sequence: an alternative approach to morpheme order." *Language Learning* 28: 175–185.

Wood, C., W. Goff, and R. Day (1971) "Auditory evoked potentials during speech perception." *Science* 173: 1248–1251.

Zaidel, E. (1973) *Linguistic Competence and Related Functions in the Right Cerebral Hemisphere of Man following Commissurotomy and Hemispherectomy.* Ph.D. dissertation, California Institute of Technology.

Zobl, H. (1980) "The formal and developmental selectivity of L1 influence on L2 acquisition." Unpublished paper.